POWER
WORDS

POWER WORDS

What You Say Can Change Your Life

JOYCE MEYER

NEW YORK   BOSTON   NASHVILLE

Unless otherwise noted, all Scripture quotations are from *The Amplified Bible*. Copyright © 1954, 1958, 1962, 1964, 1965, 1987 by The Lockman Foundation. Used by permission.

Scripture quotations marked NKJV are from the New King James Version. Copyright © 1979, 1980, 1982 by Thomas Nelson, Inc. Used by permission. All rights reserved.

Scripture quotations marked KJV are from The Holy Bible, King James Version (Public Domain).

This book is derived from material previously published in *Me and My Big Mouth* Copyright © 2002 by Joyce Meyer.

FaithWords
Hachette Book Group
1290 Avenue of the Americas
New York, NY 10104

www.faithwords.com

Printed in the United States of America

WOR

First Edition: December 2015
10 9 8 7 6 5 4 3

FaithWords is a division of Hachette Book Group, Inc.
The FaithWords name and logo are trademarks of Hachette Book Group, Inc.

The Hachette Speakers Bureau provides a wide range of authors for speaking events. To find out more, go to www.hachettespeakersbureau.com or call (866) 376-6591.

The publisher is not responsible for websites (or their content) that are not owned by the publisher.

Library of Congress Cataloging-in-Publication Data has been applied for.

ISBN 978-1-4555-8788-9

CONTENTS

PART 3
RIGHT WORDS WILL HELP YOU MAKE IT THROUGH THE MIDDLE

PART 4
LET YOUR WORDS WORK FOR YOU, NOT AGAINST YOU

PART 5
YOUR WORDS CAN DETERMINE YOUR FUTURE

Often, the seemingly small changes we make in our lives have the greatest impact. Years ago, I made a change that at first appeared small but later proved to be one of the most significant steps I ever took in my journey with God. *I changed the way I spoke.* Specifically, I changed the kinds of words I used when I talked about the things that were happening in my life. The results have been tremendous. That's why I have written this book.

I want you to understand, with God's help, that when you begin agreeing with God's Word and speaking His promises over your life, you will begin to experience a more peaceful, joy-filled, overcoming way of living.

No matter what your circumstances are, no matter how things look from a natural perspective, no matter what other people say or what your feelings may try to tell you, if you will begin speaking life—declaring God's goodness and faithfulness each day, in every situation—you will be amazed concerning the impact it will have.

Everything about your life is affected by the words you

speak—your attitude and outlook, your level of happiness, even your success. And if you'll change the words you speak so they line up more and more with God's Word, then all the other aspects of your life will change for the better, too.

According to James 3:3–5, our mouths can determine the course of our lives.

If we set bits in the horses' mouths to make them obey us, we can turn their whole bodies about. Likewise, look at the ships...they are steered by a very small rudder...Even so the tongue is a little member, and it can boast of great things.

That is a powerful picture! The words we speak can steer our lives in one direction or another. You can turn your life toward the best God has for you or settle for the best you can do on your own. It's your choice.

For years, I steered my life toward hopelessness and negativity with the words I spoke. Before I understood the incredible impact of words, I often grumbled and complained when I felt frustrated or when things simply were not going my way. I was quick to make negative, frustrated, joyless confessions with my mouth, which meant I lived a more negative, frustrated, joyless life than I should have. If you can relate to that, I have good news: You can make a change starting today and overcome negativity. You can choose to speak God's words of health and well-being, peace, joy, and His promise of life. Here is an example: I recently had a surgery and am in the process of recovering from it. One of the things I confess daily is, "God's healing power is working in me and every day I get better and better in every way." I also focus on speaking about my progress, and not merely how far I have to go. By doing this I am cooperating with God's Word, and His will can be accomplished in my life.

With God's help, you can change your words in order to change your life. As a word of explanation and caution, I am not saying you can just speak into existence anything you would like. Nor am I suggesting you deny reality with your words or lie about circumstances that are not what you would like them to be. I am talking about choosing to speak what God's Word says about your situation instead of allowing your situation or your feelings to trump what God says. Speak God's power words, and you will see His power released in your life. By speaking God's Word, we are agreeing with Him, and that enables us to walk more closely with Him and to experience His promises in our lives.

Over the years, I have come to believe that no one can experience God's very best without being well informed concerning the power of words. That's why I believe so strongly in the power of confession. I believe we should speak to our mountains (the obstacles and difficulties in our lives), and I believe that many times the answers to our problems are right under our noses, in our mouths through the words we speak. I also believe strongly in several other biblical principles in addition to understanding the power of words: the maturity of the believer, the crucifixion of the fleshly nature, laying aside selfishness, being promptly obedient to God, forgiveness, and a willingness to be led by the Holy Spirit, just to name a few.

The principles in this book are not a "formula" to get everything you want. They simply represent one more tool you can use to cooperate with God and see His great purposes accomplished in your life—and they are a "power tool"! Speaking in agreement with God is a spiritual discipline we all need to develop, and it adds power to our lives.

I believe God has an amazing life for you and it can start today. You do not have to live any longer with less than His best. Start speaking His Word—words that release His power—and watch Him do something amazing in your life.

POWER
WORDS

PART I

THE POWER OF YOUR WORDS

CHAPTER 1

Words Are Containers for Power

Proverbs 18:21 teaches us that the power of life and death is in the tongue. Words have both creative power and destructive power. Any time we have power, we also have responsibility. Many times people want some kind of power so they can play around with it or flaunt it to others, but God will not allow that. If He gives us power, He requires us to be responsible for it. Since God has given us power in our words, He wants us to be accountable for them.

In Matthew 12:36, Jesus says: "But I tell you, on the day of judgment men will have to give account for every idle (inoperative, nonworking) word they speak." If we really believe this verse and know we will have to be accountable for our words, and if we really believe our words are powerful, most of us would be much more careful about what we say.

We can be very casual in our speech, and sometimes

we say ridiculous things. If we were to record ourselves for just one week and listen to our own words, we would quickly understand why we have some of the problems we have and why some things never change.

I am sure we would hear on the recording our confessions of doubt and unbelief, complaining, grumbling, unforgiveness, fear, and words based on other negative thoughts and emotions. We would also likely hear a lot of confirmation about the negative situations that are happening to us at the time, but not much prophecy (foretelling) of the great future God has planned for us. We might hear statements such as these:

"This child of mine is never going to change! I might as well forget it. The more I pray, the worse he acts."

"This marriage is simply not going to work. I absolutely cannot put up with any more of this. If one more thing happens, I'm leaving."

"It never fails. Every time I get a little money, some problem comes along and costs me every penny I've got."

"I just can't hear from God; He never speaks to me."

"I don't care what I do, I just cannot lose weight!"

"Everyone in my family has been diabetic, so I'm just waiting for it to happen to me."

"Nobody loves me. It looks like I'm going to be alone for the rest of my life."

At the same time we are making such negative statements, we also claim that we are believing for our children, our marriage, our finances, our spiritual or physical health, and that we are believing the Holy Spirit will lead us to our lifelong mate.

Many times, we say things like these because we feel afraid or stressed. Here is an example from my life of the way I once spoke when under pressure.

One evening I was looking for something in my house and having a difficult time finding it. At the same time, various family members were asking me to help them with different things they were doing. I could feel the pressure mounting, and when the pressure gets high, the mouth flies open.

In my frustration, I blurted out, "This place drives me crazy! I can never find anything around here!"

Instantly, God called my attention to my words and led me to examine exactly what I had just said. First, I realized I had lied because I really could find things I was looking for, and most of the time I found them fairly quickly. Just because I could not find *one* thing *one* time, that did not mean I could *never* find *anything.*

Most of us tend to exaggerate when we feel pressured. We magnify circumstances, blowing them out of proportion and making them sound much worse than they really are. The careless words we speak in the heat of the moment may not mean much to us, but they definitely carry weight in the spiritual realm.

Before I said I could never find anything, I had said, "This place drives me crazy!" The Lord helped me understand that was a lie, too. I realized that my house was *not* actually going to make me go crazy, but if I kept saying it would, it just might.

If you pay attention to what people say, you will notice that a lot of individuals make negative statements about their mental capacity and condition. They say things like:

"That just blows my mind."

"I feel like I'm losing my mind."

"Sometimes I think I'm going to end up crazy."

"My brain just won't work right."

"I'm just not thinking right today."

"I never remember anything."

"I am getting so forgetful. I must be getting Alzheimer's disease!"

"If this situation does not end soon, I am going to have a nervous breakdown."

"I am so stupid!"

Just listen to the words of your own mouth and to what other people say, and you'll see what I mean.

One day years ago, my husband, Dave, and I played golf with a man who must have called himself "a dummy" a dozen times in the course of four hours. I thought, *Mister, if you had any idea how you are cursing your own life, you would stop talking like that!*

Not only do we need to stop saying such negative things about ourselves for our own good, but we also need to understand that the enemy loves this kind of talk. When we speak negatively, he rejoices because that opens a door for him to work his misery into our lives. It is important for us to see and speak about ourselves the way God does. His Word states that we have been given the mind of Christ (1 Corinthians 2:16) and therefore we should not say negative and unbiblical things about our mind and thinking processes.

If you ever do feel you are truly having some type of problem with your mind, pray about it and then start speaking good things about your mental capacity so your future can be different from what your past has been.

The apostle Paul told Timothy that God had given him a spirit of power, love, and a sound mind (2 Timothy 1:7). Paul told him this while he was enduring difficult times and was weary from various attacks on his life and on his mind. When we feel that we are mentally incapable in any way, it is good to boldly speak forth, "I have a sound mind!"

Our words do have power. I encourage you to begin right now to use them to exercise positive power over not only your mental health, but also your physical well-being and everything that affects your life and the lives of the people you love.

CHAPTER 2

Words Affect the Natural Realm

Romans 10:9–10 is a passage specifically about salvation, but it contains truths and principles that can be applied to other areas of life, too:

> If you acknowledge and confess with your lips that Jesus is Lord and in your heart believe (adhere to, trust in, and rely on the truth) that God raised Him from the dead, you will be saved. For with the heart a person believes (adheres to, trusts in, and relies on Christ) and so is justified (declared righteous, acceptable to God), and with the mouth he confesses (declares openly and speaks out freely his faith) and confirms [his] salvation.

We see in this passage the importance of both confessing "with your lips" and believing "in your heart" in the process of salvation. What we believe in our heart justifies us and makes us right with God. When we believe Christ died for us and was raised from the dead, we receive Him as Savior. But what we confess with our mouths confirms our salvation before people and before the enemy. God can see our hearts, but people and the devil hear our words. Our confession boldly declares a change of allegiance. Previously, unsaved people have served the enemy, but when salvation occurs, they give the enemy notice that they have changed masters.

The late W. E. Vine defined the Greek word translated *confirm* in the King James Version as "to make firm, establish, make secure." (W. E. Vine, Merrill Unger, William White Jr. "New Testament Section" in *Vine's Complete Expository Dictionary of Old and New Testament Words* [Nashville, TN: Thomas Nelson, Inc., 1984], p. 121.) Vine also defines the Greek word translated *confirmation* as "of authoritative validity."

In other words, confession—the speaking out of our beliefs—boldly declares what we believe and how we intend to live our lives.

The idea of confession is similar to the idea of declaring. Both involve using words to express a confident belief in, or a commitment to, something. I once saw a movie in which a king declared a royal decree. He issued a command in writing, then sent riders on horseback throughout his kingdom to "declare the decree" to the citizens. In other words, the riders declared what the king's word said. That is precisely what we are doing when we confess God's Word! King Jesus has decreed His Father's will by giving us the Bible, and we can declare by our verbal confession the decree that is in agreement with God.

In Psalm 2:7, the psalmist wrote that he would "declare the decree of the Lord." The written Word of God is His formal decree. When we believers declare God's Word out of our mouths, with hearts full of faith, those faith-filled words go forth to establish God's order and plan in our lives.

One way we declare or confess God's good plans for our lives is to call the things that are not as though they are—to believe that what we know God has promised is a reality, even if we do not yet see it in the natural realm. As believers, we learn to *"see with the eye of faith."* In other words, we believe what God says even more strongly than what we see or feel, and we speak accordingly.

In Romans 4:17, we read that God Himself "speaks of the nonexistent things that [He has foretold and promised] as if they [already] existed." In other words, He calls the things that don't exist as though they do. God called Abram *Abraham,* meaning "father of a multitude," long before Abraham had even one child. He knew His plan for Abraham and spoke about him accordingly.

Because our goal is to be like Him, we can do the same. In fact, I believe calling things that are not as though they are is one of the greatest privileges we have as God's children. For example, we can say, "All my needs are met in Jesus," before our circumstances actually change because we have seen in God's Word that He promises to meet our needs.

I want to mention that this principle works in positive ways, but it can also operate in negative ways. Calling things that are not as though they are can work against us if we are calling for things that are not God's will but the enemy's.

Sometimes I am shocked at the negative things I hear people call forth through their words. For example, a person sneezes and says, "I must be getting the flu that's going around." Or someone hears a rumor that his company plans to lay off some employees and says, "I'll probably get caught in this round of layoffs and lose my job. That's the story of my life. Every time things start to go well, something bad happens."

People who speak this way are doing much more than merely being grumpy and negative. They are actually speaking into the unseen realm and calling forth things that have not yet happened, as though they are already taking place. They are fearful concerning what is not yet a reality or a certainty, and by their negative belief and speech (because words are powerful), they are speaking words that can shape their future.

I realize that each thing we say, negative or positive, does not always immediately come to pass, but I definitely believe that if we speak negatively about things, we will have a life that is less than what we would desire. Likewise, if we speak positively on a regular basis, we will have a better life because of it.

People who have spoken negatively for years need to retrain themselves to speak positively and in line with what God says. People whose whole way of talking and relating to others has been fear based need to learn to communicate in a faith-based way. The best approach I know when trying to make that transition is to confess the Word of God—to begin using your words to speak the power of God's Word.

When I first started learning the principles I am sharing with you in this book, I was very negative. I was a Christian, and Dave and I attended church services regularly, tithed, and were active in church work. But we did not know we could do anything about any of our circumstances. We had no idea that God wanted to share His power with us or that our words were powerful.

God began teaching me that I should not think or say negative things, and I began to understand that my negativity kept Him from working in my life as He really wanted to. I came to believe I would see Him do more if I would stop being so negative. I obeyed, and before long I became a much happier person, because negative people have a hard time being happy.

After a period of time had elapsed, I did not feel my circumstances had changed. When I prayed and talked to God about this, I realized that I had stopped speaking negatively but I was not saying anything positive. That was my first lesson in calling those things that were not as though they were. God taught me this lesson in a very personal way, and it proved to be one of the major breakthroughs in my life.

As part of learning to speak by faith, I made a list of things I came to understand were rightfully mine as a believer, according to the Word of God. Twice a day for approximately six months, I confessed those truths aloud. I did this in my house all by myself, not for anyone else to see or hear. I was building my faith and growing in God while I "declared the decree." I was speaking faith-filled words into the atmosphere, and God began using them to reshape my circumstances.

I have included part of my list of confessions in Appendix A, "Confessions from the Word of God," but I encourage you to develop your own list based on your personal hopes, dreams, and needs that agree with God's Word, and on the promises of God that mean the most to you. As you are faithful in confessing the Word of God as part of your fellowship with God, it will become firmly established in your heart.

As you meditate on God's Word, which includes speaking it and rolling it over and over in your mind, it becomes part of you, and your responses to problems or difficulties in your life will change. For example, instead of blurting out of your mouth something negative when you hear a rumor of layoffs at work, you will declare that God will take care of you. He will help you keep your job, or He will get you a better one.

CHAPTER 3

Words Can Move Mountains

Do you have problems in your life? Your answer is right under your nose. At least a major part of it is. As believers, we sometimes refer to our problems as "mountains" because they operate as obstacles in our lives, and getting over them seems so difficult.

Jesus specifically told us what to do when we run into a problem or a mountain. He said, "Have faith in God [constantly]. Truly I tell you, whoever says to this mountain, Be lifted up and thrown into the sea! and does not doubt at all in his heart but believes that what he says will take place, it will be done for him" (Mark 11:22–23).

When Jesus says we are to speak to our mountains in faith, commanding them to be lifted up and thrown into the sea, He makes an unusual statement—one we need to consider in detail.

First, we need to pay attention to what we say to our mountains. In other words, when we face a problem, how do we talk to it? Notice that I ask, "How do we talk *to* it," not "How do we talk *about* it." Both are important, but right now, I want to focus on what we say to our obstacles and difficulties. Mark 11:22–23 clearly teaches us to speak God's will, not our will, and God's will is His Word. It may seem odd to think of speaking to a problem, but we should remember that Jesus spoke to storms and told them to be still (Mark 4:39).

When Satan tempted Jesus in the wilderness (see Luke 4), Jesus answered every trial with the Word of God. Jesus repeatedly said, "It is written," and quoted Scriptures that met the devil's lies and deceptions head-on.

Perhaps you have heard teaching about the power of speaking God's Word to your mountains and have tried it for a while. If you have not seen quick results, have you given up and started once again speaking your thoughts and feelings? Doing so will not bring breakthrough! We need to be persistent in doing what is right, and then and only then will we see results. It is not what we do right one time that changes our circumstances, but what we do right over and over. We must be committed to doing what is right not merely to get a result, but because it is right!

Galatians 6:9 says, "And let us not lose heart and grow weary and faint in acting nobly and doing right, for in due time and at the appointed season we shall reap, if we do not loosen and relax our courage and faint."

Only the Word of God brings the victory we need. We need to resist speaking words that originate in our minds and emotions and be persistent as we speak God's Word.

To illustrate my point about persistence, let me remind you that a stonecutter may strike a rock ninety-nine times with a hammer and see no evidence at all that the rock is cracking. Then, with the one hundredth strike, it may suddenly split in half. Each blow was weakening the stone even though the stonecutter saw no signs of the break that was only one strike away. The lesson in this example is that persistence is a vital link to victory. We must know what we believe and be determined to stick with it until we see results.

No doubt, speaking God's Word over and over, refusing to quit, is absolutely necessary to our breakthrough, but it is not the only key to overcoming our problems. Obedience is just as important. If people think they can live in disobedience to God's Word and then speak the Word to their problems and get positive results, they are mistaken; part of the power of speaking the Word also lies in a lifestyle of obeying the Word.

I believe obedience is the central theme of the Bible. Many people's lives are in a mess today because of disobedience. That disobedience may be the result of a variety of factors, including simply not knowing what God's Word says. But the fact remains that obeying the Word brings blessings, while not obeying the Word, for whatever reason, has negative consequences.

Let's look at Deuteronomy 28:1–2, which emphasizes the connection between obedience and blessings: "*If* you will listen diligently to the voice of the Lord your God, being watchful to do all His commandments which I command you this day, the Lord your God will set you high above all the nations of the earth. And all these blessings shall come upon you and overtake you *if* you heed the voice of the Lord your God" (emphasis mine). Please notice the "ifs" in this passage. They show us the importance of obedience, letting us know what we can have *if*—and only if—we listen to God and obey His voice.

God is always faithful. He is true to His Word all the time. Our disobedience does not change God, but our obedience opens the door for His blessings to flow into our lives. As believers, you and I can have what we say, but only if what we say lines up with God's Word and His will. "Speaking to our mountains" is not some kind of magic charm we can pull out and use whenever we want something as we continue in carnality and disobedience. We can speak to our problems, and our faith-filled words will move them, as long as we are living in obedience to God.

In addition to speaking God's Word persistently and walking in obedience to God's commands when facing a mountain in your life, forgiveness is crucial to breakthrough. Mark 11:24–26, which immediately follows the "speak to the mountain" passage of Mark 11:22–23, specifically addresses the relationship between answered prayer and forgiveness. It says:

> *For this reason I am telling you, whatever you ask for in prayer, believe (trust and be confident) that it is granted to you, and you will [get it]. And whenever you stand praying, if you have anything against anyone, forgive him and let it drop (leave it, let it go), in order that your Father Who is in heaven may also forgive you your [own] failings and shortcomings and let them drop. But if you do not forgive, neither will your Father in heaven forgive your failings and shortcomings.*

Mark 11:22–26 must be considered as a whole. In verse 22, Jesus says to constantly have faith in God. In verse 23, He teaches the importance of releasing faith through speaking to our mountains. In verse 24, He speaks of prayer and the importance of praying believing prayers. In verse 25, He commands us to forgive, and in verse 26, He makes the strong point that God will not forgive our failures and shortcomings if we do not forgive others. We can conclude from this teaching in its entirety that there is no power in speaking to a mountain in faith if our hearts are full of unforgiveness. We will not be successful if we try to operate in one of God's principles while completely ignoring another. Faith only works through and is energized by love (Galatians 5:6), and love requires that we forgive those who have injured us or treated us unjustly.

We all face mountains in our lives and when we do, we all want victory over them. The best way to get it is to speak God's Word persistently to your problem from a heart that lives in obedience to His Word and to put yourself in a position to have your prayers answered by living a life of forgiveness.

CHAPTER 4

Learn to Speak Power Words

When we become Christians, we have a lot to learn! For example, we need to learn what God says in His Word; we need to learn to hear His voice and obey His leading; we need to learn to pray; and we need to learn how to use our gifts and abilities to serve God and minister to others. We also need to learn to speak God's language. I encourage you to be excited about learning because the more we learn, the more powerful and fruitful our lives become.

The apostle Paul writes about this in 1 Corinthians 3:1: "However, brethren, I could not talk to you as to spiritual [men], but as to nonspiritual [men of the flesh, in whom the carnal nature predominates], as to mere infants [in the new life] in Christ [unable to talk yet]!"

We see from this verse that the more we grow up in Christ, the more we understand spiritual things. Paul was a very mature believer, and he could talk to other spiritually mature people in a certain way, whereas he needed to communicate with less mature believers in other ways.

When we first begin to walk with God, we do not have the wisdom and experience we need to say and pray for the right things all the time. When we are in this stage of spiritual growth, we should be glad God shows us mercy and does not give us everything we say! At that point in our Christian lives, we tend to say a lot of things that are based in our will, not in God's will, simply because we cannot yet tell the difference. As "mere infants" in Christ, we have not yet learned how to talk. Just as natural babies must learn to talk first as children and then in more advanced ways as adults, Christians also have to grow in learning to speak God's way.

Hebrews 5:13–14 teaches us more about maturing in God:

> *For everyone who continues to feed on milk is obviously inexperienced and unskilled in the doctrine of righteousness (of conformity to the divine will in purpose, thought, and action), for he is a mere infant [not able to talk yet]! But solid food is for full-grown men, for those whose senses and mental faculties are trained by practice to discriminate and distinguish between what is morally good and noble and what is evil and contrary either to divine or human law.*

Maturity takes time. We know it takes time physically, but it also takes time spiritually. We need time to get to know God, to learn His Word, and to know His heart.

When we think about speaking in agreement with His Word, we realize that His will for some things is clearly expressed in His Word (salvation, healing, Christlikeness, and wholeness, for example).

When I was less mature in my walk with God and knew less of His Word, I often took principles I learned to an extreme. For example, when I began learning that my words had power, I began to make positive confessions about things I wanted, without considering if they were God's will for me. We can know much of God's will by studying His Word, but there are many decisions we need to make that are not precisely covered in God's Word. For example, the Word doesn't tell me when to purchase an automobile or what kind to purchase. It doesn't tell me what career choice to make or who to marry. In these types of decisions, I must be led by the Holy Spirit and by His wisdom and peace. We can and should pray for and fully expect God to fulfill the promises He clearly makes in His Word, and to give us all other things in His timing and in ways that are right for us to have.

People may hear that they can have what they say, but we can only have what God says we can have. Our goal is to learn to live in agreement with God. Many years ago I heard that people of faith can "have what they say." I liked that principle because I wanted what I wanted and thought I had finally found a new and easy way to get it. But I did not understand that concept fully. I was taught half of a truth, which in reality is no truth at all.

I needed to grow up and mature in my faith in order to understand the fullness of the power of words and what it really meant to "speak to my mountains," "declare the decree," and "call those things that be not as if they already existed."

Asking with Humility

James 4:2 says we do not have certain things because we do not ask God for them. The following verse, James 4:3, says that sometimes we ask and fail to receive because we ask for the wrong purpose or with selfish motives. That may be hard for us to believe about ourselves, but it is still true at times. It is especially true of believers who have not allowed God's purification process to take place in their lives. In that condition, people definitely have God living in their hearts, but they are carnal Christians rather than spiritual Christians.

I believe that in those instances, when what we are asking God for is not clearly spelled out in God's Word and we are not positive we have clear direction from Him about a matter, the wise thing to do is pray, "If it is Your will." This way, we can pray boldly about what we would like, but we are also submitting ourselves to what God wants. We are praying with humility and saying we only want the things we are requesting if they are what God wants for us.

Many years ago, Dave and I were vacationing in a lovely

place in Georgia. We were extremely tired, and God had made a way for us to take some time off to be refreshed and restored. We were enjoying the place so much that we started planning to return to that same vacation spot the following year and take our children with us for an extended family vacation. We were so excited about our plans, and I began to "declare" (make a verbal confession of faith), "We are coming back to this place next year and our entire family will be blessed with a vacation here."

Suddenly, I felt a strong prompting to remember James 4:15, which says, "You ought instead to say, If the Lord is willing, we shall live and we shall do this or that [thing]." I later began to study that passage of Scripture and noticed verse 16: "But as it is, you boast [falsely] in your presumption and your self-conceit. All such boasting is wrong."

There is a difference between faith and confidence, and foolishness and presumption. Until we discern that difference, our spiritual lives can be full of striving and disappointment instead of filled with grace and victory.

Praying with humility sounds like this: "Lord, I would like this thing—*if* it is Your will, *if* it fits in with Your plan, *if* it is Your best for me, and *if* it's Your timing." In fact I often pray, "God, please don't give me anything I ask for if it is not the best thing for me according to Your will."

Proverbs 3:7 teaches us not to be wise in our own eyes. In other words, we should not think we know best. God is the only one who really knows what is best for us and when is the perfect timing for us to receive it.

There was a time in my life when I thought I knew everything and believed that if everyone would listen to me, we would all get along just fine. I have now discovered that I don't know nearly as much as I once thought, certainly not compared to what God knows. I am hungry to learn and grow spiritually every day.

PART 2

CHANGING YOUR WORDS IS PART OF SPIRITUAL GROWTH

CHAPTER 5

Your Words Reflect Your Disposition

Webster's defines the word *disposition* as "one's usual mood; temperament," "habitual tendency or inclination," or "usual manner of emotional response" (*Webster's II New College Dictionary* [Boston: Houghton Mifflin Company, 1995], s.v. "disposition"). One way people identify our disposition is through our words.

What kind of disposition do you have? Are you basically happy and good-natured, or are you usually grumpy or grouchy? Are you sweet and kind, or are you sour and mean? Are you even tempered, or do you become angry easily? Are you positive and upbeat, or are you negative and depressed? Are you easygoing and easily pleased, or are you harsh and demanding?

In my early years I seemed to be surrounded by people with negative dispositions. People who are that way are very difficult to please. If you have ever been around people with such negative tendencies, I'm sure you know what I mean. They are never satisfied with anything. They always seem to want something other than what they have—like sitting down to a meal of fried chicken and expressing their disappointment that the chicken is fried instead of baked. That's a simple example, but it makes my point.

As believers, we need to have positive, faith-filled dispositions. In fact because we are God's beloved children, created in His image, He wants us to have the same soothing disposition that His Son Jesus displayed. Many of us believe that if Jesus walked into a room full of strife, it would only take Him a few minutes to bring peace to that situation. He had that kind of soothing nature. He was clothed with meekness (Matthew 11:29). He wasn't out to prove anything, and He was not concerned about what people thought of Him. He already knew Who He was, so He didn't feel the need to defend Himself. Though other people sometimes got upset with Him and even tried to lure Him into arguments, His response was always peaceful and loving.

Jesus wants our dispositions and our words to have that same soothing effect on people. He also wants us to use our words to encourage and build people up everywhere we go.

In order to grow in Christ, we have to ask ourselves whether our disposition is similar to His or not. Are we humble, simple, and agreeable, or are we proud, complicated, and rigid?

My husband, Dave, is one of the people I have known who truly has a soothing disposition. He is so easygoing it is amazing to me. He can be ready to lie down and take a nap, and I can ask him to do something for me and he almost always seems to be willing to change his plan without murmuring about it.

If someone asked me to run an errand, or do something for him or her just as I was ready for a nap, I doubt my disposition would be quite as pleasant! But I am thrilled to say that with God's help I have improved a lot, and I expect to continue doing so.

Some people who have soothing dispositions are encouragers. No matter what is going on around them or what others are saying or doing, they always seem to have a word of affirmation or kindness to share with everyone.

Proverbs 8:6–9 is a powerful passage of Scripture, full of principles we should aim for in our speaking:

> *Hear, for I will speak excellent and princely things; and the opening of my lips shall be for right things. For my mouth shall utter truth, and wrongdoing is detestable and loathsome to my lips. All the words of my mouth are righteous (upright and in right standing with God); there is nothing contrary to truth or crooked in them. They are all plain to him who understands [and opens his heart], and right to those who find knowledge [and live by it].*

This passage should be not only our confession and testimony, but also our reputation. That is, it should be not only what we say about ourselves, but also what others say about us.

Can you imagine having someone say about you what these verses say? In today's language, he or she might say something like this: "She [or he] speaks such excellent things! She speaks the truth and hates wrongdoing. Everything she says is in right standing with God. There is nothing deceitful or false in the words of her mouth. When she speaks, everything is clear. She is easy to understand and people always learn from her."

As admirable as this description is, it does not fit as many people as it should. However, we should all aspire to it. Unfortunately, many of us have learned to talk in circles. When we finish speaking, often others still don't know exactly what we have said. We need to learn how to engage in plain, straightforward, honest, truthful communication.

As we read in James 3:10, blessings and cursings, or good and evil, should not both come from our mouths. Instead, like the virtuous woman in Proverbs 31, kindness should be on our tongues. As children of God, filled with His Spirit, we are to express the fruit of the Spirit through our words and actions, especially kindness, gentleness, meekness, and humility (Galatians 5:22–23). Those virtues are to characterize our disposition.

That is the way God intends for us to be. That is what He gave us our mouths for—not to belittle people or to judge others or to criticize and condemn those who dis-agree with us.

As people who love God and want to serve Him, you and I are not to be harsh, hard, or unbending. We are to be soothing, kind, encouraging, and humble. If these traits are in our hearts and minds, they will inevitably express themselves through our mouths.

CHAPTER 6

Is Your Mouth Saved?

I well remember the day I came to the realization that my mouth needed to be saved. You may think that sounds a little strange, so let me explain.

Once I became a believer, I was saved. But it is possible to be a Christian and not act like one or speak like one. A person can definitely be a child of God, yet not sound like part of God's family. I know that because in my early years as a believer, I was one of those people. That's when I learned that simply receiving Jesus as Lord in my heart was only the beginning of my journey with God and that according to His Word I also needed to "work out" my salvation with fear and trembling.

Once salvation takes place in our hearts, our minds, mouths, attitudes, behavior, and other areas need to be saved, so to speak, too. This is part of the sanctification process that every child of God goes through.

Work out (cultivate, carry out to the goal, and fully complete) your own salvation with reverence and awe and trembling (self-distrust, with serious caution, tenderness of conscience, watchfulness against temptation, timidly shrinking from whatever might offend God and discredit the name of Christ).

Philippians 2:12

In addition to writing these words in Philippians, Paul also wrote the book of Ephesians. In Ephesians 2:8–9, he clearly stated that salvation cannot be earned, that it is a gift of God's grace; it is received through faith and is not some kind of reward for good works: "For it is by free grace (God's unmerited favor) that you are saved... not because of works..." In these two portions of Scripture, the apostle teaches us that we are not saved by our "works," but that we do need to "work out" our salvation.

Let me explain: The free gift of salvation is given to us totally by God's grace and is not in any way based on anything we do. We receive by faith! When we receive the free gift and we are saved or born again, we also receive the Holy Spirit who undertakes the job of helping us "work out" the free gift of salvation we have received. This process is called *spiritual maturity*, and it is very important. Far too many Christians remain baby Christians. They don't grow and mature, and as a result they are unable to be useful to God in furthering His Kingdom.

When we receive Jesus, He creates within us a new heart. This is something that only God can do, and He does it through His grace, mercy, love, and goodness. He does all the work, and we receive the free gift by faith.

We then enter into a lifelong process of becoming more and more like Jesus. We begin to "work out" our salvation, but thankfully we don't do it in our own strength (Philippians 2:13). We might look at the process as being similar to what happens when a seed is planted in the ground and later becomes a fruitful plant. Salvation is like a seed planted in our hearts. Once it is deposited, then we need to cooperate with the work of the Holy Spirit to see that the seed He has placed in us grows into a plant—strong, healthy, vibrant, and productive.

Jesus is the Seed of everything good that God desires for us to become, experience, accomplish, and enjoy. God Himself plants the Seed through His gift of salvation, but we must cultivate it, nurture it, water it, and care for it as the Holy Spirit leads us. We must also allow Him to help us keep the ground in which the Seed is planted plowed and free from weeds.

The ground where the Seed is planted is a metaphor for our lives. Keeping that ground weed free and plowed means we need to cooperate with God as He changes us in ways we need to change and removes things that need to be eliminated from our lives. This does not happen all at once; it takes time. There is a great work to be done, and only the Holy Spirit knows how and when to accomplish the work. As we study God's Word and submit to Him, He will change us into Christ's image (2 Corinthians 3:18).

If you and I were to think back to the early days of our walk with God and take an inventory of the things He has changed in us since that time, we would be amazed at all He has done. We could easily see how different we are now than we were when we first started our lives as Christians.

As a young believer, one of the areas in which God first dealt with me was the area of independence. Because of certain aspects of my upbringing, I was an extremely independent person, and I sensed that God was challenging me to learn not to do anything without leaning on Him.

After working on my independence for a while, God began to deal with me about other things. I remember a period of time when He focused on my motives and started teaching me that what I did was not as important as why I did it. He also worked with me on my attitude, my entertainment choices, the way I dressed, my thoughts—and, of course, my mouth.

I have to say that He has probably dealt with me more consistently about my mouth than about any other issue. He knows that words contain the power of life or death, and He wants you and me to speak life. Just this morning in my fellowship time with God, He gave me a refresher lesson in the power of gratitude. He reminded me how important it is to use my words to voice thankfulness instead of to complain or murmur. So after all these many years of walking with God, He is still dealing with me about my mouth!

God has called me to teach His Word, and it is important that my mouth is not a fountain that puts out both sweet and bitter water (see James 3:11). No matter what God has called you to do, chances are it will involve your words in some way. Even if you are not called to public speaking, you will most likely use your mouth as your primary means of communicating with others. If you use words wrongly, confusion, hurt, and misunderstanding can result. But if you use your words well, you can bring hope, encouragement, wisdom, and life to any relationship or any situation.

God may deal with you about your words as He did me. Is your mouth saved? If you need to make progress in being more accountable for your words, ask God to help you and get started right away making progress. God will help us clean up any foul language or filthy talk that may have been a part of our life before we were saved, and He will deal with us concerning any talk that does not agree with His Word.

We will learn to speak faith and not fear, and confidence instead of doubt. We will learn to speak words that contain God's power and that agree with His will. If we speak according to His Word, our words will be based on His promises, which include speaking words of love and encouragement to others, and words of healing, strength, provision, protection, abundance, confidence in Him, and hope for the future, among many other good things.

CHAPTER 7

God Cleanses an Unclean Mouth

The prophets—Isaiah, Jeremiah, Hosea, Ezekiel, Jonah, and others—were mouthpieces for God. They were called to speak God's words to people, situations, cities, dry bones, mountains, or whatever God told them to speak to. To fulfill their God-ordained missions, they had to be completely submitted to the Lord. Not only did their hearts and minds need to be in submission to God, but their mouths also had to be His.

God still uses submitted people to speak messages to others. Those messages may be extremely important, with the ability to change the course of a nation, a church, a business, or a family; they may also be simple words of encouragement, wisdom, knowledge, confirmation, or even direction. God's Word states that we can speak a word in due season to the weary (Proverbs 25:11).

Some people may be called to teach God's Word and preach to large audiences, while others are gifted to share simple truths from Scripture with friends or coworkers. The size of the audience is not important. What's important is that we learn to be faithful with what God gives us to do and obedient to His leading. Whatever words He calls us to speak, we want to be ready to speak them. Every person can be used daily to speak words to others that will bring blessing to them.

God spoke powerfully through the prophet Isaiah, but he had to deal with Isaiah's mouth first. I know God had to cleanse my mouth before He could use me as He desired, and perhaps God wants to use you in a greater way, but He needs to cleanse your mouth first! When God called Isaiah, He gave him a dramatic vision. Isaiah actually saw the Lord sitting on His throne and heard the angels crying, "Holy, holy, holy is the Lord of hosts; the whole earth is full of His glory!" (Isaiah 6:3).

In response, Isaiah said, "Woe is me! For I am undone and ruined, because I am a man of unclean lips, and I dwell in the midst of a people of unclean lips; for my eyes have seen the King, the Lord of hosts!" (Isaiah 6:5). It is interesting to me that when Isaiah was in the Presence of God, the first thing he noticed was that he had unclean lips.

Notice what happens next:

Then flew one of the seraphim [heavenly beings] to me, having a live coal in his hand which he had taken with tongs from off the altar; and with it he touched my mouth and said, Behold, this has touched your lips;

your iniquity and guilt are taken away, and your sin is
completely atoned for and forgiven.

Isaiah 6:6–7

After the angel touched Isaiah's mouth, God Himself
spoke to Isaiah with a question: "Whom shall I send? And
who will go for Us?" and Isaiah answered, "Here am I;
send me" (Isaiah 6:8). God then gave Isaiah some instructions: "Go and tell this people..." (Isaiah 6:9).

God's call to Isaiah is an excellent example of the fact
that God often needs to cleanse people before He uses
them. Ponder the progression of this story: Isaiah has a
vision of God and immediately when he recognizes God,
he also recognizes that he is a man of unclean lips. As
soon as he recognizes and admits his sin, God cleanses
his mouth and announces forgiveness. Then God asks
whom He could send on a mission and Isaiah cries out,
"Here am I; send me," and God tells him to go and speak
His words to the people.

I find this fascinating, perhaps because I am called to
teach the Word and have been through a similar process
in my own life.

We are all born with a sin nature, and though salvation
makes us a new creation, we still need to put off the old
man and put on the new (Ephesians 4:22–24).

We see from Isaiah 6:1–9 that when we come into God's
presence, He will deal with us. In Isaiah's case, Isaiah
himself realized and admitted that he had an unclean

mouth. I believe the cry of his heart was to change and clean up his mouth, so God sent help.

No matter what our sin is, whether we have an unclean mouth like Isaiah, a fearful mouth like Jeremiah (which I will elaborate on in the next chapter), or something else, God always has forgiveness available to us. First John 1:9 says,

> *If we [freely] admit that we have sinned and confess our sins, He is faithful and just (true to His own nature and promises) and will forgive our sins [dismiss our lawlessness] and [continuously] cleanse us from all unrighteousness [everything not in conformity to His will in purpose, thought, and action].*

First John 1:9 is a New Testament example of what God did for Isaiah in the Old Testament. He forgave and removed Isaiah's sin, cleansing his lips, just as He promises to forgive the sin we confess and "cleanse us from all unrighteousness."

Isaiah had a perfect heart toward God even though he had some imperfection in his actions. God always looks for people whose hearts are perfect toward Him, not for people whose performances seem perfect or who seem to do everything right. When God knows He has a person's heart that is loyal to Him, He also knows He can work with that person to make the necessary changes in thoughts, words, or behavior.

Second Timothy 2:21 says, "So whoever cleanses himself [from what is ignoble and unclean, who separates himself from contact with contaminating and corrupting influences] will [then himself] be a vessel set apart and useful for honorable and noble purposes, consecrated and profitable to the Master, fit and ready for any good work."

This truth should be a great encouragement to those of us who want God to use us, but feel we have too many flaws. As the saying goes, "God uses cracked pots." All we have to do is come to Him as we are, with a willing, humble heart, and He molds us and makes us into people He can use, just as He did Isaiah.

CHAPTER 8

Preparation for Greater Things

Those of us who desire for God to use us need to allow Him to deal with us concerning our words, just as Isaiah did. We need God to teach us to speak differently than we have spoken in the past, so our words line up with His words, His thoughts, and His character.

In this chapter, I want to highlight the prophet Jeremiah. Like Isaiah, he spoke powerfully for God.

God did not speak through Jeremiah until *after* He had dealt with him concerning his mouth. Just as Isaiah and Jeremiah had to go through a process of correction and preparation to speak what God wanted them to say, we also have to learn how God wants us to speak. These two men had problems that are still common for many believers today. As you read in the last chapter, Isaiah had an unclean mouth, and you will see in this chapter that Jeremiah had a fearful mouth. I believe many of us can relate to one or the other of them, or to both of them. As we see how God transformed the way they spoke, we can learn valuable lessons on the way to handle our own words.

I hope you will read carefully the following passage from God's Word because it will give you the background necessary to understand why God had to work with Jeremiah's mouth before He could use him.

Then the word of the Lord came to me [Jeremiah], saying, Before I formed you in the womb I knew [and] approved of you [as My chosen instrument], and before you were born I separated and set you apart, consecrating you; [and] I appointed you as a prophet to the nations. Then said I, Ah, Lord God! Behold, I cannot speak, for I am only a youth. But the Lord said to me, Say not, I am only a youth; for you shall go to all to whom I shall send you, and whatever I command you, you shall speak. Be not afraid of them [their faces], for I am with you to deliver you, says the Lord. Then the Lord put forth His hand and touched my mouth. And the Lord said to me, Behold, I have put My words in your mouth. See, I have this day appointed you to the oversight of the nations and of the kingdoms to root out and pull down, to destroy and to overthrow, to build and to plant.

Jeremiah 1:4–10

Right after God called Jeremiah as "a prophet to the nations" (Jeremiah 1:5), Jeremiah immediately began to say things God had *not* told him to say. God's words affirmed His call to Jeremiah and His belief in him, but as soon as He finished speaking, Jeremiah began to confess his doubt and weakness because of his young age (Jeremiah 1:6). God had to straighten out Jeremiah's fearful mouth before He could use him. That was part of God's process of preparation for Jeremiah, and He will have to prepare us in similar ways to speak for Him.

We must understand that when God calls us to do something, we should not say that we cannot do it. If God says we can do it, then we can! So often we speak out of our insecurities, or we verbalize what others have said about us, or we give words to what the enemy has put into our minds. We need to stop doing those things and start saying about ourselves what God says about us.

Jesus makes an important comment about the words He speaks in John 8:28 and 12:50, which we can paraphrase this way: "I speak not My own words, but the words of the One Who sent Me. I say only what I have heard My Father say."

God is calling us up higher. He is challenging us to no longer speak our own words. He wants us to speak His words because He wants to use us for His purposes. No one is ever used without preparation. That means God must deal with us, and we need to allow Him to do everything He needs to do *in* us, so He can do everything He wants to do *through* us.

Some people are new believers and God is just now

starting to do His work in them. Others have been walking with Him for years, and now is a time for some fine-tuning. He has been working in their lives for years in general ways, and now He is making some precise adjustments in order to release them to their next level.

Regardless of where we are on our spiritual journey, I believe God is calling all of us to a new place, and every time we step up to a new level of blessing and being used by God, we face new opposition. Jeremiah had spoken one way before God called him, but once he received God's new assignment for him, his speech had to change. The way he once spoke would have gotten him into trouble as he began to carry out God's plan for his life.

Wrong words can open doors we do not want to open for the enemy. We don't want to give the devil even a tiny crack, let alone an open door! One way to eliminate those opportunities is to be careful with our words.

God intended to use Jeremiah to prophesy to the people some powerful things that would convict them of sin and bring victory for God and defeat for the enemy. Instead of opening doors for the enemy, God wants us to speak such powerful words of faith that we will do damage to the kingdom of darkness.

God wants to use all of us, and this is a time when He is dealing with people to let go of childish ways and be strong men and women of God. Paul said when he was a child he talked like a child, reasoned like a child, and thought like a child, but once he became a man he was done with childish ways (1 Corinthians 13:11). I think this should be our attitude also. It is time to lay aside childish ways, and that means we can no longer say whatever we feel like saying, but we realize the power of our words and become accountable for them.

Once God dealt with Jeremiah's mouth, He used him in mighty ways. In fact, He spoke through Jeremiah a verse that has encouraged millions of believers over the years and given hope to people who were tempted to give up. I pray it will encourage you today. "For I know the thoughts and plans that I have for you, says the Lord, thoughts and plans for welfare and peace and not for evil, to give you hope in your final outcome" (Jeremiah 29:11). This should give us great confidence for the future!

If you are struggling with fear, as Jeremiah once did, and you find yourself speaking doubt-filled words, remember that God was faithful to Jeremiah. God dealt with Jeremiah to the point that He could entrust him to write the words I just gave you from Jeremiah 29:11, which have changed lives for generations. He will be faithful to deal with you, too, and to prepare you for the great things He has planned for your life.

PART 3

RIGHT WORDS WILL HELP YOU MAKE IT THROUGH THE MIDDLE

CHAPTER 9

Cross Over to the Other Side

Some of the most difficult times for us to discipline our thoughts and words are when we find ourselves in the storms of life—the major challenges; the big problems; the times when we are very fearful, hurt, disappointed, or confused; or when we feel threatened or have experienced some kind of loss. We all experience the storms of life to varying degrees, we all have our faith tested and tried, and we all must learn how to live—including how to use our thoughts and words to help us, not hurt us—in the midst of the storm.

Scriptures such as John 14:30 and Isaiah 53:7 have always intrigued me, but I had no real understanding of the message they convey until the Holy Spirit revealed to me that they are related to our mouths and to the storms we face in life. The first Scripture is something Jesus said; the second is a prophetic word about Jesus from the Old Testament:

I will not talk with you much more, for the prince (evil genius, ruler) of the world is coming. And he has no claim on Me. [He has nothing in common with Me; there is nothing in Me that belongs to him, and he has no power over Me.]

John 14:30

He was oppressed, [yet when] He was afflicted, He was submissive and opened not His mouth; like a lamb that is led to the slaughter, and as a sheep before her shearers is dumb, so He opened not His mouth.

Isaiah 53:7

We see from Isaiah 53:7 that when Jesus was experiencing the most intense pressure of His life, He decided it would be wise not to open His mouth. Why? I believe He knew that in His humanity He would have been tempted to speak the same way you and I would want to speak under such stressful conditions—to doubt, question God, complain, or make negative comments.

Under extreme pressure, even the strongest, most mature believers can say things they shouldn't if the stress is high enough and goes on long enough.

Jesus is the Son of God, Himself God, but He came to us in the form of a human being. The writer of Hebrews says in Hebrews 4:15 that He "was in all points tempted as we are, yet without sin" (NKJV).

I believe that when our Lord was faced with trying

situations in which He knew He might be tempted to say things that would not be fruitful, He chose not to open His mouth. He purposefully decided not to say anything at all. He was able to be quiet when He needed to be.

This is a wise decision for anyone to make during times of stress. Instead of speaking out of emotions that are in turmoil or out of wounded feelings, we are smart to allow our emotions to subside before we say anything. That way, we will avoid saying things that may not honor God or won't express our faith and trust in Him, and we will not stir up negativity within ourselves with our words.

Jesus and His disciples encountered a fierce storm on the Sea of Galilee one day. This was a natural storm, but we can learn some lessons about facing the storms of life from their story. Their trip across the lake started when Jesus said, "Let us go over to the other side [of the lake]" (Mark 4:35). To me, this sentence is equivalent to Jesus saying, "I have something new and great for you," or "Let's experience a new blessing," or "Promotion is coming," or any of the variety of phrases the Lord may use to communicate to us that a change is on its way. I am sure the disciples were excited about finding out what was going to happen on the "other side." What they probably did not expect was a raging storm on the way! You have probably noticed in your life that not all storms are in the forecast.

Mark 4:37–38 describes what happened on their voyage: "And a furious storm of wind [of hurricane proportions] arose, and the waves kept beating into the boat, so that it was already becoming filled. But He [Himself] was in the stern [of the boat], asleep on the [leather] cushion; and they awoke Him and said to Him, Master, do You not care that we are perishing?"

The disciples were not nearly as excited in the middle of their trip across the lake as they had been in the beginning.

Although God often calls us to launch out into something new, He usually does not let us know what is going to happen on the way. We leave the security of where we are and head for the blessings of the other side, but in the middle, we often encounter the storms. The middle is often a place of testing.

The storm was in full force, and Jesus was asleep! Does that sound familiar? Have you ever had times when you felt that you were sinking fast—and it felt to you that Jesus was asleep? You prayed and prayed and heard nothing from God. You spent time with Him and tried to sense His presence, and yet you felt nothing. You searched for an answer, but no matter how hard you struggled against the wind and the waves, the storm raged on—and you didn't know what to do about it.

The storm the disciples faced was no harmless summer thundershower, but a storm "of hurricane proportions." The waves quickly filled the boat with water, and the disciples were genuinely afraid, as anyone would be.

At times like this, when our boats seem to be sinking with us in them, we must use our faith. We can talk about faith, read about it, hear sermons on it, or sing songs about it. But in the middle of a storm, we must use it. Also, at times like this, we discover just how much faith we really have.

Faith, like muscle, grows stronger with use. Every storm we go through equips us to better handle the next one. Soon we become such good navigators that the storms don't disturb us at all. We have been through them before and we already know how they will end: Everything will be all right. Once we believe that, we can say with confidence that we will reach the other side.

CHAPTER 10

Talk to Yourself

As powerful as words are when you speak them to other people, they are just as powerful when you speak them to yourself, especially when you are going through a difficult time. Sometimes, there are certain things you really need to hear, but no one around you is saying them. What do you do when that happens? You speak those words to yourself.

One of the Bible's best examples of this is in 1 Samuel 30:6, when David needed encouragement: "David was greatly distressed, for the men spoke of stoning him because the souls of them all were bitterly grieved, each man for his sons and daughters. But David encouraged and strengthened himself in the Lord his God."

I can certainly relate to David's situation, and I'm sure you can, too. We have all had times when everyone around us had nothing but negative things to say, and their words only served to make us feel worse than we already felt. We may have also had times when we could not talk about specific circumstances as much as we wanted to, and therefore felt alone. No one knew about our problem, so no one could encourage us.

At other times, we may not have many people in our lives who truly understand what we are going through, so no one realizes how much we need to be encouraged. I can relate to that somewhat. In my ministry, especially in the early days, there were many times when I felt so discouraged and down in the dumps that I just wanted to give up and quit. It seemed I had no one to encourage me in the specific ways I needed encouragement.

I became so "weary in well doing" (Galatians 6:9, KJV)—with hard work, study and preparation, raising children, trying to lay an excellent foundation for a new ministry, and thinking about the endless decisions that had to be made—that I frequently found myself physically, mentally, and emotionally exhausted.

I truly needed and wanted someone to encourage me at that time, but I did not feel that anyone really understood what I was going through. At times I became angry because there was no one to encourage me, and I ended up thinking about how hard I was working for everyone else while others did very little for me. I was sinking into a pit of resentment, and that is a dangerous place to be. The way I felt wasn't anyone else's fault and it was useless to blame them. Their encouragement would have been refreshing, but I look back now and realize that God wanted me to totally trust Him and go to Him for what I needed.

Have you ever felt that way? Do you know what that kind of thinking does? It fills the soul with bitterness and resentment. And when our souls are full of that kind of negativity, then bitter, resentful words come out of our mouths. This is not the way the Lord wants us to respond to situations that cause us to feel pressured, discouraged, and worn out. He wants us to come to Him to find our strength and encouragement.

I finally learned to do that. I realized that if I would go to God in earnest, humble prayer and use my words to talk to Him instead of being angry or resentful and using my words to complain, things would get much better for me. When I learned to say, "Lord, I need to be encouraged, and I trust You to bring it the way You choose," then I received cards, phone calls, flowers, and other gifts as ways through which people expressed their encouragement. In fact, people seemed to go out of their way to speak kind words of affirmation and support to me. But every time I allowed myself to get resentful and complain about the lack of encouragement in my life, things only got worse.

Right now, you may be feeling that no one cares about you, that no one appreciates you. I would urge you to be careful not to take that too personally. It's possible people simply do not understand your need. Maybe the reason some people don't seem to appreciate you is that they are excessively busy or pressured right now, or they are consumed with a family situation that requires all their energy. Perhaps they do not receive much encouragement in their lives, so they do not think to encourage others. Or, and unfortunately this does happen, they are self-centered and really do not know how to appreciate others. If you become bitter and resentful or speak negatively (even to yourself) about the people you wish would encourage you, chances are that you will never receive what you desire from them. In fact, bitterness and resentment will eat away at you and could end up destroying your relationships with those people.

But if you will take your burdens to the Lord, He will hear you, help you, and send you the very person or people you need to uplift, support, and edify you. So the first thing to do when you need encouragement is to pray.

The second thing to do is to sow encouragement. Don't just sit around waiting for someone to encourage you; start encouraging other people. By all means, don't refuse to encourage someone who needs a good word simply because you are not being encouraged. Step out and give other people what you wish someone would give you— and you will soon reap a harvest of encouragement for yourself.

The third thing to do when you need encouragement is to be like David and strengthen and encourage yourself. If you are working hard at something you know God has called you to do, even if it's difficult at times, remember that God has called you and remind yourself of that. Say to yourself, "God has called me to do this, and even though I'm challenged right now, He is in it. He is helping me do what He wants me to do. He is a faithful God, and He will bring this to completion."

In addition, remind yourself of the many truths in God's Word. Tell yourself how much God loves you. Speak to your own soul and tell it to hope in God. Say over and over again to yourself that God fights your battles for you and always leads you in triumph (1 Samuel 17:47; 2 Corinthians 2:14). At the end of this book, you will find several Scriptures you can use to encourage yourself. If you will meditate on them and speak them with your own lips, they will chase away any discouragement you may feel and fill you with courage, confidence, and faith.

We must never forget how powerful our own words are in our lives. Always remember Proverbs 18:21. I know I have mentioned it several times in this book, but it bears repeating here: "Death and life are in the power of the tongue, and they who indulge in it shall eat the fruit of it [for death or life]."

When we think about the *power* of the tongue, we can view ourselves as going through life with an awesome force—like fire, electricity, or nuclear energy—right under our noses. This power can produce life or death, depending on how it is used. With this power, we have the capacity for great good or for great evil, for great benefit or great harm. We can use it to create death and destruction, or we can use it to create life and health. We can speak forth sickness, strife, bitterness, and all kinds of negative things, or we can speak forth healing, harmony, peace, encouragement, and all kinds of positive things. We can do this for others and for ourselves.

When you feel down or discouraged, remember the tremendous power that is in your own mouth, and use it for your good.

CHAPTER 11

Have Faith—and Echo God's Words

Romans 8:37 says we are more than conquerors. To me that means we know we will win before the battle ever starts. When God calls us to a new place, we can be confident we will get there, even if we have to face a storm along the way. In order to reach our goal, we do have to go through the storm, which is not always fun, but we know that in Christ we will be victorious.

Faith is for the middle of a situation. Starting something does not require tremendous faith, nor does reaching the finish line once the end is finally in sight. The beginning and the end are both exciting, but the middle can be rough. Yet we all have to go through the middle to get to the other side.

When the disciples found themselves tossed about on the stormy sea, Jesus wanted them to believe what He had told them. We saw in chapter 9 that He had said, "Let us go over to the other side." He expected them to believe that if He said it, it would happen. But as is often the case with us, they were afraid once they found themselves up against a storm.

Jesus calmed the storm, but He rebuked the disciples for their lack of faith (see Mark 4:39–40). The lesson we can learn from this situation is that we must grow in faith and learn to press through the storms of life and reach the other side. We need to improve in our response to the challenges we face, and we can start by disciplining our mouths. In the storms of life, we must speak God's Word and resist the temptation to talk about our doubts and fears. For a believer, the truth about any difficulty in life is that God will get us to the other side, and our words need to line up with that truth.

Psalm 119:1 says, "Blessed (happy, fortunate, to be envied) are the undefiled (the upright, truly sincere, and blameless) in the way [of the revealed will of God], who walk (*order their conduct and conversation*) in the law of the Lord (the whole of God's revealed will)" (emphasis mine).

We must "order" our conversation in accordance with God's will. When you find yourself in a time of trial, try not to look just at where you are right now and what is happening at that moment, but rather see yourself and your circumstances through the eyes of faith. You have cast off from the shore, and now you may be in the middle of the sea with the storm raging, but you will get to the other side. Blessings are waiting for you there, so don't give up, and begin to say what God says. Instead of saying, "I'm never going to make it through this storm," say, "I already have the victory."

Many people get discouraged and backslide during challenging times, and part of the reason they do so is that they never learned what to say in the midst of a storm. They never learned how to use their words to help them, not to harm them, on their life's journey.

A trial is discouraging in and of itself; we don't need to add insult to injury by depressing ourselves or bringing more despair to a situation that feels hopeless through negative speech.

It is common when enduring trials, especially ones that are long standing, to feel frustrated and not know what to do. I have learned that when I don't know what to do, the best thing to do is to keep doing what I do know. I may not know how to solve my current problem, but I do know how to pray, to be thankful for what I have, to be a blessing to others, to keep my commitments, to study God's Word, and other things.

Deuteronomy 26:14 gives us a good example of how our human emotions operate and how the enemy works when we face the storms of life. In this verse, the Israelites were commanded to present their offerings to the Lord and say to Him, "I have not eaten of the tithe in my mourning..."

Sometimes when people are mourning or facing great challenges, they begin to eat their own tithe (withhold from God what is due Him) instead of giving it to the Lord, thereby backsliding in their giving. Why? Because being obedient to the Lord is harder in times of difficulty than in times when things are going well.

In this example about tithing, the enemy comes and whispers to the person in despair, "This tithing business is not working, so you better hold on to what you've got instead of giving it away." Then the mouth says, "That's right. This isn't working. I'd better use my money to meet my own needs because no one else is helping me."

I believe the same principle this situation teaches about tithing also applies to many other areas, including the way we use our words. When hardships arise, we are often tempted to listen to the enemy's lies and echo his words instead of staying strong and speaking God's words. The enemy does not want us to get through our difficulties to the other side. In fact, he does not want us to make any progress at all. He will whisper discouraging, depressing words in our ears, and if we listen to them instead of recognizing them as lies and resisting them, we will begin to agree with them and repeat them.

Jesus made a similar observation in the parable of the sower in Mark 4. The ground in this story represents different kinds of hearts that receive God's Word. In Mark 4:17, He came to the seed sown on stony ground and commented about the people that ground represented: "And they have no real root in themselves, and so they endure for a little while; then when trouble or persecution arises on account of the Word, they immediately are offended (become displeased, indignant, resentful) and they stumble and fall away."

Jesus recognized that people can stumble or grow weak in their faith during times of trial and tribulation. He encourages us in John 16:33:

I have told you these things, so that in Me you may have [perfect] peace and confidence. In the world you have tribulation and trials and distress and frustration; but be of good cheer [take courage; be confident, certain, undaunted]! For I have overcome the world. [I have deprived it of power to harm you and have conquered it for you.]

These are the things we need to remember and speak!

CHAPTER 12

Tame the Tongue

James 3:10–11 says, "Out of the same mouth come forth blessing and cursing. These things, my brethren, ought not to be so. Does a fountain send forth [simultaneously] from the same opening fresh water and bitter?"

These verses encourage us to eliminate "double talk," which means saying one thing in good times and another in hard times. If you have ever known anyone who spoke with confidence and enthusiasm at the beginning of some kind of situation, then started speaking negative, doubtful words when facing a storm in the middle, then you know what double talk sounds like. As believers, we need to speak sweet words, not only during good times, but also during periods of difficulty when we are tempted to speak bitter words. It's not always easy to discipline our speech in this way, but it's very important. As God's Word instructs, we can and should *order* our conduct and conversation according to God's will.

Jesus, in His humanity, was subjected to the same

pressures and temptations we have; yet He was not up and down emotionally, nor did He just speak positively when things were going well and negatively when facing hardships. According to Hebrews 13:8, He stayed the same and was steady all the time: "Jesus Christ is the same yesterday, today, and forever" (NKJV). I am sure He had to discipline His mouth during the storms He faced, and we are to follow His example and do the same. This kind of control over our tongues is a sign of maturity and it is a way we can glorify God.

In James 1:26, we learn that no matter how many good deeds we do, they are worth nothing if we cannot tame our tongues: "If anyone thinks himself to be religious (piously observant of the external duties of his faith) and does not bridle his tongue but deludes his own heart, this person's religious service is worthless (futile, barren)."

As you can see, James makes a very strong statement. He is saying that we can do all kinds of good works that could be attributed to our religious convictions, but if we do not "bridle" our tongues (meaning, to discipline our mouths), our good deeds are futile. This kind of warning from Scripture should make us take even more seriously the issues of our words, how we speak, and how we use our mouths.

If you have ever seen a bridle on a horse, you know that the bridle is a harness that goes on a horse's head and includes a bit, which goes over the tongue and reins attach to it. The rider either relaxes or pulls on the reins to guide or restrain the animal. To "bridle the tongue" simply means to control our mouths.

The image of the bit is not new in the New Testament. Even the Old Testament psalmist understood the connection: "Be not like the horse or the mule, which lack understanding, which must have their mouths held firm with bit and bridle, or else they will not come with you" (Psalm 32:9).

A horse either follows the pull of the reins, which controls the bit in its mouth, or it experiences great pain. Our relationship with the Holy Spirit works in a similar way. He is our bridle and the bit in our mouths. He should be controlling the reins of our lives. If we follow His promptings, we will end up at the right places and stay out of all the wrong places. But if we do not follow Him, we can end up in painful situations. Especially when we are in the midst of life's storms, if we don't bridle our tongues we may never reach the breakthrough God has for us or experience the fullness of His plan for our lives. But if we will accept the leadership and guidance of the Holy Spirit, He will act as a bridle and bit for us, leading us where we should go and helping us know what to say.

The image of a horse and bridle is powerful when we think about how it applies to taming our tongues, but James uses another image that also helps us understand the impact of the words we speak. He compares the tongue to the rudder of a ship in James 3:3–5:

> *If we set bits in the horses' mouths to make them obey*
> *us, we can turn their whole bodies about. Likewise,*
> *look at the ships: though they are so great and are*
> *driven by rough winds, they are steered by a very small*
> *rudder wherever the impulse of the helmsman deter-*
> *mines. Even so the tongue is a little member, and it can*
> *boast of great things. See how much wood or how great*
> *a forest a tiny spark can set ablaze!*

This passage indicates that the tongue sets the direction for our lives just as the rudder of a ship sets its direction.

The tongue is such a small member of the body, but it can accomplish major things. It would be wonderful if all those things were good, but they are not. The tongue can ruin relationships. In fact, sometimes couples even get divorced over things they have said to each other. Words can be terribly wounding, and some people never recover from hurtful comments others have made. The tongue may be a small part of the body, but oh, how powerful it is! Let us remember that the power of life and death are in the tongue!

Over the years, I have had to learn a lot of lessons about the power of words, and I have had to discipline my mouth. When I encourage you to tame your tongue, I am not asking you to do anything I have not also had to do. I need help with my mouth every day. I pray Psalm 141:3: "Set a guard, O Lord, before my mouth; keep watch at the door of my lips."

When I pray the words of this verse, I am inviting the Holy Spirit to convict me when I am talking too much, when I am saying something I should not say, when I am speaking negatively, when I am complaining, when my words sound harsh, or when I am speaking doubt or fear-filled words. These things all fall under the category the Bible calls "evil speaking" (1 Peter 2:1) and they are offensive to God.

Anything that offends God needs to be eliminated from our conversation. That's why we need to continually pray Psalm 141:3, asking God to set a guard over our mouths and keep watch at the door of our lips.

Another Scripture I pray regularly is Psalm 19:14: "Let the words of my mouth and the meditation of my heart be acceptable in Your sight, O Lord, my [firm, impenetrable] Rock and my Redeemer."

One of the best ways I know to speak words that are filled with power is to pray, asking for God's grace and help. James said that no man can tame the tongue (James 3:8), and it is clear that without God's help in this area we will totally fail.

Let Psalm 141:3 and Psalm 19:14 be the cry of your heart concerning your words. If you are sincere in your desire for your words to line up with God's Word and bring God's power into your life, you will soon see the changes you want to see as you ask Him to help you guard your lips and have your thoughts and words be acceptable to Him.

In addition, I want to share with you a prayer of

commitment for exercising control over your mouth. This prayer has certainly helped me, and I believe it will help you, too:

> *Lord, I pray that You will help me develop sensitivity to the Holy Spirit concerning all of my conversation and every word I speak. I do not want to be stubborn, like a horse or mule that will not obey without a bridle and bit. I want to move in the direction in which You would have me go, with only a gentle nudge from Your Spirit.*
>
> *During the storms of life, while I am crossing over from one side to the next, I ask for Your help. I always need Your help, Lord, but times of stress and pressure bring unusual temptations to sin with my words.*
>
> *Place a guard over my lips and let all the words of my mouth be acceptable in Your sight, O Lord, my Strength and my Redeemer. In Jesus' name I pray, amen.*

CHAPTER 13

Talk Like a Prisoner of Hope

Everyone encounters some kind of storm in life at some point. Throughout the Bible, men and women faced the same types of difficulties you and I face today. The culture they lived in was very different from modern-day society, so some of the details were different, but the emotional impact of their challenges was as intense for them as it is for us.

In this chapter, I want us to look at three specific storms people faced in Bible times, one in the Old Testament and two in the New Testament, and learn from them how we need to speak during hard times.

Let's look first at the story of the dry bones in Ezekiel 37:1–4:

The hand of the Lord was upon me, and He brought me out in the Spirit of the Lord and set me down in the midst of the valley; and it was full of bones. And He caused me to pass round about among them, and behold, there were very many [human bones] in the open valley or plain, and behold, they were very dry. And He said to me, Son of man, can these bones live? And I answered, O Lord God, You know! Again He said to me, Prophesy to these bones and say to them, O you dry bones, hear the word of the Lord.

You may feel as though your life is no more than dead, dry bones. Maybe your circumstances are so dead you feel they are decaying. Your hope may seem lost, but God has a way out.

If you continue reading in Ezekiel 37, you will see that the prophet follows God's instructions and sees God totally revive what was dead and bring breath and spirit back into a pile of dry bones (vv. 5–10).

The same thing can happen to you and me, but not unless we learn to speak God's Word. The key to the dry bones that came to life was that Ezekiel spoke to them as God led him (vv. 7, 10). If we want to see God's power through our words, we can no longer speak idle words or allow our mouths to say whatever they want to when we are under pressure. We must speak what God says to speak.

In the Gospel of John, Jesus' good friend Lazarus became ill and his sisters asked Jesus to come to him:

Now a certain man named Lazarus was ill. He was of Bethany, the village where Mary and her sister Martha

lived. This Mary was the one who anointed the Lord with
perfume and wiped His feet with her hair. It was her
brother Lazarus who was [now] sick. So the sisters sent
to Him, saying, Lord, he whom You love [so well] is sick.

John 11:1–3

John 11 records the whole story of Lazarus's illness and
eventual death. By the time Jesus arrived on the scene,
Lazarus had been dead for four days. Going out to meet
Jesus, the dead man's sister Martha said to Him, "Master,
if You had been here, my brother would not have died"
(John 11:21). Later, her sister Mary said exactly the same
thing to Him: "Lord, if You had been here, my brother
would not have died" (John 11:32).

I can sympathize with the sisters and you probably
can, too. We all feel at times that Jesus could have helped
us if He had only been with us in a certain situation. We
feel that had He only shown up sooner, things would not
have been so bad. For example, I am sure the disciples felt
their circumstances would have been better had Jesus not
been sleeping in the bottom of the boat when the storm
seemed to threaten their lives (see Mark 4:37–38).

In John 11:23–25, we see how Jesus responded to Mary's
and Martha's words of hopelessness and despair:

Jesus said to her, Your brother shall rise again.
Martha replied, I know that he will rise again in
the resurrection at the last day. Jesus said to her, I am

*[Myself] the Resurrection and the Life. Whoever believes
in (adheres to, trusts in, and relies on) Me, although he
may die, yet he shall live.*

You may know the rest of the story: Jesus called Lazarus, a man who had been dead for four long days, to come
forth from the tomb, and he did so, totally restored. If
Jesus can raise a dead man, surely He can raise a dead
circumstance.

We can see from Ezekiel's experience with the bones,
and from the story of Lazarus, that no matter how bad
things seem, God will make a way. But remember, there are
spiritual laws we must respect in order to see the miracle-
working power of God. A great illustration of one of these
laws is in the story of the woman with the issue of blood:

*And there was a woman who had had a flow of blood
for twelve years, and who had endured much suffering
under [the hands of] many physicians and had spent
all that she had, and was no better but instead grew
worse. She had heard the reports concerning Jesus, and
she came up behind Him in the throng and touched His
garment.*

Mark 5:25–27

The woman with the issue of blood had been having the same problem for twelve years. She had suffered
greatly, and no one had been able to help her.

Surely, thoughts of hopelessness had consumed this woman. Whenever she thought about going to Jesus, she must have heard, "What's the use?" But she pressed on past the crowd that was so thick around Jesus on all sides that it must have been suffocating. She touched the hem of Jesus' garments, and healing power flowed to her and she was made well (paraphrase Mark 5:29–34, AMP, KJV).

We don't want to miss this aspect of her story, from Mark 5:28: "For she kept saying, If I only touch His garments, I shall be restored to health." Do you see the important part of her comment? She *kept saying*. She *kept saying*. She did not stop; she *kept saying*.

No matter how she felt, no matter how much others tried to discourage her, even though the problem was twelve years old and the crowd looked impossible to get through, this woman got her miracle. Jesus told her that her faith had made her whole (see Mark 5:34). How was her faith released? Through her words.

In order for faith to work, it has to be activated, and one way we activate it is through our words. Whenever you face a problem, even if it has been a problem for a long time, activate your faith with your words. Say what God says—and keep saying it.

We have considered three "storm stories"—dry bones that came to life, a dead man brought back to life, and a long-term, incurable disease totally cured. All three of these storms were impossible for human beings to calm or correct, but with God all things are possible (see Matthew 19:26).

Years ago, Dave and I went through a certain storm and the Holy Spirit led me to a Scripture I had not seen before. It was as though He had hidden it like a treasure, just waiting to reveal it at a time when I would really need it. It is Zechariah 9:12: "Return to the stronghold [of security and prosperity], you prisoners of hope; even today do I declare that I will restore double your former prosperity to you."

As "prisoners of hope," we must be filled with hope, we must think hope, and we must talk hope. Hope is the foundation on which faith stands.

Some people try to have faith after having lost all hope, and that doesn't work. Refuse to stop hoping no matter how dry the bones may seem, how dead the situation may appear, or how long the problem has been around.

God is still God, and Zechariah 9:12 teaches us that if we will remain positive and be "prisoners of hope," God will work miracles on our behalf.

PART 4

LET YOUR WORDS WORK FOR YOU, NOT AGAINST YOU

CHAPTER 14

Complain and Remain

We can use our mouths for good or bad. Our words can help us in life or they can hurt us. One of the best things we can do with our mouths is to speak words of praise and thanksgiving to God, which I will elaborate on in the next chapter. One of the worst things we can do is complain.

I believe complaining is a major problem among believers. It has gotten so bad that sometimes we ask God to give us something, and when He answers our prayer, we complain that we have to take care of the thing we asked Him to give us. We must treat the temptation to complain like the plague, because it has similar effects in our lives. Complaining weakens us, whereas praise and thanksgiving strengthen and empower us.

Many people think it's normal to complain when we encounter something we do not like or enjoy, but the Bible makes it clear that complaining is a sin. Jesus Himself said, "Do not murmur among yourselves" (John 6:43, NKJV), and the apostle Paul wrote: "Do all things without complaining and disputing" (Philippians 2:14, NKJV). In addition, the Old Testament includes a number of passages about the dangers of complaining, especially for the Israelites who complained a *lot* (Exodus 16:8; Numbers 11:1–4, 21:4–6; Psalm 106:25).

Paul wrote in Ephesians 4:29: "Let no corrupt word proceed out of your mouth, but what is good for necessary edification, that it may impart grace to the hearers" (NKJV). A complaint is a "corrupt word," and conversations that involve complaining are built on corrupt words and cause many people a great deal of trouble in their lives.

You know by this point in the book that words are containers for power. Complaining, grumbling words carry destructive power. They destroy the joy of the person who complains and can negatively affect the people listening to the complaining.

Murmuring and grumbling are like verbal pollution, and pollution can eventually become poison. You and I can actually poison our future by complaining about what is going on in our lives right now. When we complain in our current circumstances, we remain in them. But when we praise God in the midst of difficulty, He raises us out of it.

First Corinthians 10:9–11 is an eye-opening passage about the negative power of complaining. It describes what happened when the Lord's people complained in the wilderness:

We should not tempt the Lord [try His patience, become a trial to Him, critically appraise Him, and exploit His goodness] as some of them did—and were killed by poisonous serpents; nor discontentedly complain as some of them did—and were put out of the way entirely by the destroyer (death). Now these things befell them by way of a figure [as an example and warning to us]; they were written to admonish and fit us for right action by good instruction, we in whose days the ages have reached their climax (their consummation and concluding period).

When we complain, God takes it personally. He considers that we are speaking against His goodness. God is good, and He wants to hear us praise and thank Him for His goodness and to use our words to tell others about it. When we murmur, grumble, and complain, we are giving a "critical appraisal" of the God Who loves us.

The Israelites exploited God's goodness and complained, and the Bible says they were "put out of the way entirely by the destroyer." Both the Old and New Testaments record this for our instruction (1 Corinthians 10:9–10; Numbers 16:41, 49; 21:4–6), so we can take note of their mistakes and not make the same ones. The result of the Israelites' complaining was death and destruction. We need to remember and understand that God takes complaining seriously, and be diligent to pray for God's help, and watch our mouths so we do not complain.

People who guard their words can keep themselves from ruin, but those who are not careful about what they say can bring destruction into their own lives. Proverbs 21:23 says, "He who guards his mouth and his tongue keeps himself from troubles," and Proverbs 13:3 says, "He who guards his mouth keeps his life, but he who opens wide his lips comes to ruin."

When the Israelites went into the wilderness, God repeatedly had to deal with them about complaining. The journey they needed to take from Egypt to the Promised Land should have taken about eleven days (see Deuteronomy 1:2), but after forty years the Israelites were still wandering in the wilderness of death and destruction. One reason their journey took so long was because they could not stop complaining about the difficulties of their travel.

On the other hand, Jesus went to the cross to pay for our sins and even while He was suffering terribly He didn't complain. He was raised from His situation in three days. So we see that the Israelites complained and remained in their situation for forty long years, but Jesus praised and was raised in three days.

This is a great lesson for us. We should diligently guard against the temptation to complain and grumble, and instead choose on purpose to offer God sincere words of praise and thanksgiving. We would do well to challenge ourselves daily not to complain about anything. This does not mean we deny the existence of problems, but it does mean we search for the good in everything and exalt it above the bad. We can always find a reason to be thankful no matter what is going on in our lives. Complaining does no good at all. It doesn't move God to help us, and it doesn't cheer us up while we are waiting for our deliverance. I want to be the most thankful person on the planet and I know that it is going to be challenging, but all things are possible with God!

CHAPTER 15

Praise and Be Raised

God's Word has so much to say about the uplifting power of praise and thanksgiving, and I believe these two things combined make the antidote for the poison of complaining. The best way to start every day is with words of gratitude and thanksgiving. If you don't fill your thoughts and conversation with good, positive things, the enemy will try to fill them with bad, negative things.

The world is full of two forces, good and evil. The Bible teaches us that good overcomes evil (Romans 12:21), so we must choose the good. If we find ourselves faced with a negative (evil) situation, we can overcome it with good. Complaining and grumbling are evil and negative, whereas praise and thanksgiving are positive and good. Complaining weakens us, but praise and thanksgiving strengthen us.

Truly thankful people do not complain. They are too busy being grateful for the good things they do have that they do not have time to notice things they could complain about.

The writer of Hebrews instructs us to be thankful all the time: "Through Him, therefore, let us constantly and at all times offer up to God a sacrifice of praise, which is the fruit of lips that thankfully acknowledge and confess and glorify His name" (Hebrews 13:15). We should not just praise God and offer thanksgiving when we feel we have a reason to do so. Praising and giving thanks is easy when we have a reason, but Hebrews 13:15 says we are to offer a *sacrifice* of praise. The sacrifice comes in when we think we have no reason to be thankful but we voice our thanks and praise anyway. The Israelites under the Old Covenant offered the sacrifice of dead animals, but we can offer a living sacrifice of thanksgiving! Our words of gratitude come up before God as a sweet-smelling sacrifice.

We should offer praise and thanksgiving at all times, being mindful to thank God for all the blessings in our lives and for the favor He has shown us. If we started making a list of our blessings, we would quickly see that we have so much for which to be thankful. I have tried to make a list of all the things I am thankful for, and to be honest I get tired of writing before I am finished and usually stop somewhere along the way. In America, we take many things for granted because we have an abundance of them, but people in other countries would think they were wealthy if they had them.

For example, think about clean, fresh water. In many parts of the world, clean water is a commodity that is not easy to come by. Some people must walk miles just to get a one-day supply of it. But in America, we take baths in clean water; we swim in it; we wash our dishes with it; we use it to do our laundry; we water our plants with it; we drink it; we cook with it; and we do all kinds of other things with it, including waste it. We can have it hot or cold, as often as we like, as much as we want. But this is a luxury that is not available in many places. Have you ever thanked God for water?

Another thing I am thankful for on a regular basis is that I sleep great at night. I have had times when I haven't slept well, and I have talked with people who never sleep good and it is a miserable, wretched thing. How about thanking God that you can walk, talk, hear, and see if you are able to do all of these things. There are many people who cannot and would love to just be able to get out of bed without assistance.

There are many things to be thankful for if we decide we will be people who continually offer our praise and thanksgiving to God. The flesh looks for things to complain about, but the spirit searches for reasons to give God glory.

In Philippians 2:14, the apostle Paul warns us, "Do *all* things without grumbling and faultfinding and complaining [against God] and questioning and doubting [among yourselves]" (emphasis mine).

Then in 1 Thessalonians 5:18 he exhorts us, "Thank [God] in *everything* [no matter what the circumstances may be, be thankful and give thanks], for this is the will of God for you [who are] in Christ Jesus [the Revealer and Mediator of that will]" (italics mine).

In Ephesians 5:20, he writes that we should give thanks *"at all times* and *for everything*...in the name of our Lord Jesus Christ to God the Father"* (italics mine).

From these Scriptures we see that not only are we to avoid grumbling, faultfinding, complaining, questioning, and doubting, but we are also to give thanks "at all times" in every circumstance "for everything." God does not bring bad things into our lives, but when we remain thankful even in the midst of them, it honors and glorifies Him greatly. It also lets the devil know that his defeat is imminent because it is impossible to keep a thankful person in bondage.

We testify to the goodness of God in a major way when we refuse to complain in the middle of a circumstance in which the people around us think we have every right to murmur and grumble. When people realize we are going through a difficult time and even say things like, "Wow, this must be really hard for you," it makes an impression on them when they hear us speaking words of thanksgiving to the Lord. It's a good witness, it uplifts them, and it gives God glory.

I am especially fond of Philippians 2:14–15, which instructs us to do everything without complaining that we may show ourselves to be blameless in the midst of a wicked generation. It says we are to be bright lights shining out clearly in a dark world. Think about it: In the world today, we hear murmuring and complaining everywhere we go. People who have jobs murmur about the boss or the circumstances of their job, or their pay, while people who don't have jobs murmur because of their unemployment. The list of complaints is endless. It includes the government, housing, health, people in our lives we find fault with, the weather, traffic, and on and on. Let us make a decision to get out in the world and be different. Let us outdo the complainers! Surely we can find more to be thankful for than wicked people can find to complain about.

Let me encourage you to not only refuse to complain, but to also choose to be thankful and praise God in every situation. You will have to do this on purpose, because it goes against human nature. You will not always feel like praising God, but if you will make a decision to do it anyway, you can release power in your life. For years, I have said, "The praising life is a powerful life," and I believe that now more than ever.

I encouraged you in the previous chapter to challenge yourself to live every day without complaining. Now I want to encourage you to add a second part to that challenge. Don't just refuse to complain every day, but also determine to be thankful and to praise God every day. Try going to bed at night pondering your blessings and thinking of all the things you are thankful for. Let prayers of thanksgiving be the first words you speak every morning.

Be sure to thank God not only for the "big" things He does in your life, but also for the many "little" things He does for you.

Getting into the habit of being thankful and expressing your thanks with your words every day will help you develop an attitude of gratitude. Don't be discouraged if you have a bad day and forget to be thankful; just start over the next day—and pretty soon, you will become a powerful, praising person who rises above your circumstances.

CHAPTER 16

Resist Harsh, Angry Words

Let's take a look at an important Scripture about the mouth, Ephesians 4:31:

> Let all bitterness and indignation and wrath (passion, rage, bad temper) and resentment (anger, animosity) and quarreling (brawling, clamor, contention) and slander (evil-speaking, abusive or blasphemous language) be banished from you, with all malice (spite, ill will, or baseness of any kind).

All the descriptive words in Ephesians 4:31 identify things that get us into trouble. What a list! It includes bitterness, bad temper, resentment, contention, and abusive language, just to name a few. I believe all of these things are rooted in pride and self-centeredness. In other words, these things come up in us because we do not get what we want when we want it. These things come up in everyone at times. No one is perfect, and no one has perfect attitudes and behavior all the time. So I wonder, which of these pose the biggest problem for you?

For me, I would have to say that some of the biggest problems I dealt with in the past were a bad temper and resentment. I used to have a terrible temper and get excessively angry. I was also resentful due to abuse in my childhood and feeling I didn't get a good start in life. Thankfully, with God's help I have been delivered from both of these, but I still deal with selfishness and impatience on a daily basis. Both of these weaknesses affect how we treat people. It is God's will that we truly love all people, and love is seen in how we treat others. It is not merely a word, or a theory, but it is action. I have decided that I want to treat people well, and since that is the case, then I must let God deal with me and deliver me from anything and everything that prevents me from doing so.

No one has to have a bad temper or be quick to anger. No one has to be hard or harsh toward other people. We don't have to be selfish or impatient. The Holy Spirit will help us overcome these ungodly traits if we sincerely want to change. It may take time and determination, but God will change us if we ask Him to.

The Bible teaches us in James 1:19 to be "quick to hear [a ready listener], slow to speak, slow to take offense and to get angry." Of these, the most important—and often the hardest part—is being slow to speak. Once we open our mouths and start speaking without forethought or self-control, we are going to cause problems or hurt someone.

One of the times in life that we tend to get cranky is when we have our plans made and something comes along to disrupt them. When that happens to me, I have learned to take a deep breath and consider what to say and what not to say before I do anything else. Learning to think before we speak is a wise way to live. Individuals who speak rashly always end up causing trouble with their words.

Things never go exactly as we had planned day after day, and we have to learn how to adapt to people and situations (Romans 12:16). Another way to say it is that we need to learn to "go with the flow." This statement has more meaning to me than it may for most people because of some incidents that happened often in our household when my children were very young. Seemingly, *every* time we sat down for a meal, someone spilled a glass of milk. Whenever that happened, I got upset. I immediately flew into a rage, saying things like, "I don't believe it! Look what you did! I spent all afternoon preparing this meal, and you have just ruined it!"

Really, no one in the family was ruining the meal except me. I thought the problem was the spilled milk, but it was actually the spoiled me.

In those days, we had big meals with lots of dishes and utensils all over the table. When a glass of milk spilled, it invariably started running right under all those dishes and utensils. The milk would head straight for the crack in the top of our table—the place where we could expand the table by adding a leaf when needed.

The reason I was so upset about the milk reaching the crack was that I knew once it did, it would run down the table legs and under everyone's feet. When that happened, I would not only have a milk spill to clean up on the table-top, but I would also have to take apart the table, clean the crack (where lots of crumbs and dirt accumulated anyway, making a bigger mess), and then get down on my hands and knees and crawl under the table to clean its underside and to wipe up the spill on the floor.

As I mentioned, this scenario happened often when our children were small. One of them would spill the milk or some other liquid, and the minute it happened, they all knew what my reaction was going to be, and it wasn't one of self-control and patience.

I would jump up from the table, complaining all the way, and run to get a rag. I would crawl under the table on all fours, usually with someone kicking me in the head because the space under the table wasn't huge. I was *not* a "happy homemaker." In fact, I would get so angry I felt that I was going to explode.

When we are caught in a situation we cannot change no matter what we do, that's when we need to learn acceptance with joy.

"Acceptance with joy"; that's a sweet-sounding little phrase, but it is much harder to do than to talk about doing it. It took a long time, but I eventually learned how foolish it is to get upset over things I cannot control. Once something like this happens, no amount of anger is going to reverse it, so we need to learn to adapt and deal with it.

I did not know how to do that when I first started diving under the table to catch milk spills. I just had emotional fits—yelling and screaming—acting like a grown-up little brat.

During one of those scenes, the Holy Spirit impressed on me that all the fits in the world would not get the milk to run back up the table legs, back through the crack, back across the table, and back into someone's glass. In other words, He was letting me know my temper tantrums were not going to reverse my problem.

We need to understand that no matter how angry we get or how impatient we may be, throwing a fit will not change anything. It may, however, give you a headache, a neck ache, an upset stomach, a rash, high blood pressure, and eventually a nervous breakdown. The question is: Are all those angry words really worth saying?

I finally learned—after a lot of unnecessary, unhelpful, angry responses—to go with the flow and not lose my peace. When I do that, nicer words come out of my mouth and I help preserve a peaceful, pleasant atmosphere for myself and for those around me. As the parent, I needed to set the example for my children of how to behave when accidents happen. It took a while, but God finally gave me a breakthrough and I was able to apologize to my children, and actually, over the years, we have had a lot of laughs recalling my "under-the-table excursions."

CHAPTER 17

Put the Law of Kindness on Your Lips

Many people are familiar with Proverbs 31, which describes a virtuous, or godly, woman. Verse 26 of that chapter says, "She opens her mouth in skillful and godly Wisdom, and on her tongue is the law of kindness [giving counsel and instruction]."

One of my biggest problems in learning to control my anger and my harsh words was the fact that in the early years of my life, I had been mistreated and abused. As a result, I ended up with a harsh, hard spirit. As a young adult, I was determined that no one was ever going to hurt me again, and that attitude permeated my thoughts and influenced my speech.

Though I tried to say things that were right and pleasing to others, by the time those comments had passed through my soul (my mind, my will, and my emotions) and picked up the hardness and bitterness hidden there, they came out sounding harsh and impatient.

No matter how right people's hearts may be before the Lord, if they have pride, anger, or resentment in their spirit, they cannot open their mouths without somehow expressing those negative traits and feelings. They may not even recognize the harshness in their tone of voice, but others do.

Jesus gave us the reason why we cannot keep our thoughts and emotions from influencing our words: "Out of the fullness (the overflow, the superabundance) of the heart the mouth speaks" (Matthew 12:34). Whatever is in our hearts will come out in our words.

Because I spent years as a harsh, angry person, the Lord had quite a bit of work to do in me in order for me to develop gentleness and patience. In fact, cultivating gentleness became a key issue in my life. Part of what God revealed to me in His Word concerning this issue was Proverbs 31:26. When I read it, I thought, *Oh, Lord, I've got anything but the law of kindness on my tongue!* I felt I was so hard inside that whenever I opened my mouth, out came a hammer.

Before God dealt with me about being gentle and developing kindness in my tone of voice, my words sounded terrible. I could not even tell my children to take out the trash without coming across like a drill sergeant. Who wants to live with a person like that? I know it was hard on my family, but it was hard on me, too. I did not want to be that way, irritable and impatient all the time. My father had behaved that way, and although I hated the way he had made me feel, I found myself doing the same thing to others.

Maybe you can relate to what I experienced. You may have been mistreated and abused as a young person, as I was, and you have ended up full of hatred, resentment, distrust, anger, and hostility. Instead of kindness, you express harshness and hardness, even when you do not want to.

If this is the case, I can tell you from experience that while that kind of person is not pleasant for anyone to be around, you are making yourself more miserable than you are making anyone else. Spending time in God's Word and in fellowship with Him, letting Him bring healing to the hurts of your past, getting counseling if you need it, and working to overcome the negativity you have grown up with are worth the effort. When the law of kindness is on your tongue, not only will the people around you benefit, but you will also feel better about yourself and be more able to enjoy your life.

Jesus speaks such comforting and encouraging words in Matthew 11:29–30:

Take My yoke upon you and learn of Me, for I am gentle (meek) and humble (lowly) in heart, and you will find rest (relief and ease and refreshment and recreation and blessed quiet) for your souls. For My yoke is wholesome (useful, good—not harsh, hard, sharp, or pressing, but comfortable, gracious, and pleasant), and My burden is light and easy to be borne.

I believe part of what Jesus was talking about when He told us to take His yoke upon us is to willingly submit our hearts—especially the hurts and wounds from the past, and the harsh words that resulted from those wounds—to His will and His way. We cannot tame our own tongues (James 3:8), but the Holy Spirit will help us control them. He will lead us to the healing we need in order to speak gracious words to ourselves and others, and to put the law of kindness on our lips.

When I first began to allow the Holy Spirit to help me become a kinder, more gentle person, I looked up the word *gentle* in *Strong's Concordance*. When I read what it meant, I said, "Lord, You have got to help me!" I truly thought there was no way I could ever be gentle.

I struggled as God began to work in me concerning gentleness because, like many people, I was such an extremist that I could not find a happy medium. Once I saw I was unbalanced in a particular area of my life, I thought I had to go as far as possible in the other direction. When God was teaching me to be gentle, I became so gentle and kind for a while that I let my youngest son get away with almost anything. I almost stopped disciplining him altogether because I did not want to sound harsh.

I also went overboard in my relationships with other people. I was reluctant to speak up when I felt something was not right, and I was hesitant to offer corrections or suggestions for improvement when needed because I did not want to come across as unkind. I let some things get out of balance in the ministry. My problem was that I became so accommodating and understanding that I was ineffective when dealing with people or situations that legitimately called for a firm hand.

I learned from those experiences that one extreme is as bad as the other. In an effort to not be harsh, I had become not gentle, but weak! We should not be irritable and impatient, but at the same time, we cannot be so mild mannered that we become doormats for those who might want to take advantage of us. The key is balance.

Over time, God taught me how to be a gentle person who knows how to be firm when necessary. Generally speaking, I have learned to keep the law of kindness on my tongue and to be patient with people. When situations call for me to take a stronger position, I can do so and I am comfortable in it. But I am thankful that I am no longer harsh, hard, and angry all the time. I do have a firm, straightforward personality, and I don't need to pretend to be something that I am not. But no matter what kind of personality we have, we are still required to be like Jesus.

If you have struggled to be kind and gentle for any reason, I hope this chapter and my personal testimony offer encouragement to you. I am living proof that radical change is possible in this area, and I am confident that if you will ask and allow the Holy Spirit to lead you, He will transform you in a wonderful way.

CHAPTER 18

Speak No Evil

Proverbs 15:4 says: "A gentle tongue [with its healing power] is a tree of life, but willful contrariness in it breaks down the spirit." The principle in this verse is the same as the one in Proverbs 18:21, which says we minister either life or death with our mouths: "Death and life are in the power of the tongue."

These two verses explain why God's Word reminds us so often to pay attention to the words we speak. In Ephesians 4:29, Paul writes: "Let no foul or polluting language, nor evil word nor unwholesome or worthless talk [ever] come out of your mouth, but only such [speech] as is good and beneficial to the spiritual progress of others, as is fitting to the need and the occasion, that it may be a blessing and give grace (God's favor) to those who hear it."

Notice that the word *spirit* in Proverbs 15:4 is spelled with a lowercase "s." This tells us the verse is not talking about the Holy Spirit, but refers to the human spirit. In other words, our words have the power to give life or to break down the spirits or hearts of other people, as well as our own. Thinking about the three Scriptures I have mentioned so far in this chapter, we can conclude that as believers, we are not to speak things that would discourage people and make them want to give up in life, nor are we to pollute ourselves or others with negative words or comments. We are not to use our mouths to hurt, break down, or discourage people; rather, we are to speak words that heal, restore, and uplift. Try giving each person you come in contact with a sincere compliment! People light up when we highlight something good about them.

In every situation, we have a choice. We can use our words to be a positive influence or a negative one. In most situations, and in most people, we can find something good and something bad. Every day we live, we will be satisfied and pleased with some things, but not pleased with everything. Romans 12:21 teaches us how to deal with negative things in a positive way: "Do not let yourself be overcome by evil, but overcome (master) evil with good." God wants us to focus on the good—not the bad—in life, in others, and in ourselves. We need to choose to do this continually so it becomes a habit in the way we speak.

The reason we need to be so diligent and deliberate about speaking positively is that many of us have spent years speaking negatively. That negative speaking comes from negative thinking. I believe many of us actually have mental strongholds of negativism that need to be destroyed so we can think and speak positively.

A stronghold is like a brick wall built in our minds. It gets constructed one brick at a time—one thought at a time—as we rotate certain kinds of thoughts through our minds. We could say that by thinking certain thoughts again and again over a period of time, we develop ruts in our thinking. Once established, those ruts, or habitual ways of thinking, become very difficult to change. But until those strongholds are destroyed, they will cause us trouble. Let me give you an example.

I once counseled a young woman who had a terrible self-image. She felt so badly about herself because all of her life, people had repeatedly told her she was no good and would never amount to anything. The older she got, the more she replayed that message in her head. For years, she said to herself, "I am no good. I will never amount to anything. There must be something wrong with me. If I were okay, people would love me and treat me right." Because of the lies she believed, which created ruts in the way she viewed herself, she struggled in relationships and in other areas of her life.

I understood this young woman's challenges and I knew how the strongholds had been built in her life because I had developed them in my own life. I have mentioned many times that for years I was very negative in my thinking and in my speech. The reason I had such a stronghold of negativism was that so many negative things happened to me during my early life and so many negative things were said to me and about me.

I grew up in a negative environment—surrounded by negative people who looked at things in negative ways. Because I spent so much time in that atmosphere of negativity, I learned to be negative, too. For years, I did not know I had a choice. By the time I was an adult, I felt I was protecting myself by having a negative outlook on life. I thought that if I did not expect anything good to happen to me, I would not be disappointed when it didn't.

If you think about the people you know, you may realize that good things tend to happen to people who expect good things and have a positive attitude toward life. The opposite is also true. Negative people tend to draw negative circumstances. Even if circumstances themselves are not entirely negative, a pessimistic person will view them that way and speak negatively about them.

Over the years, I have met lots of negative people. Like me, they were raised in negative environments so they now have a negative spirit. Those kinds of people are not a joy to be around, and they are no joy to themselves. But there is a way to avoid being negative and to destroy and overcome strongholds of negativity.

One way you can get started right now to destroy strongholds of negativity is to meditate on and apply Philippians 4:8 to your life. In this verse, Paul talks about what to think and gives us a list of things we should think about:

Whatever is true, whatever is worthy of reverence and is honorable and seemly, whatever is just, whatever is pure, whatever is lovely and lovable, whatever is kind and winsome and gracious, if there is any virtue and excellence, if there is anything worthy of praise, think on and weigh and take account of these things [fix your minds on them].

One thing I have said in ministry for years is this: "Think about what you're thinking about." In other words, do not let the enemy fill your mind with the thoughts he wants you to think or allow random thoughts to cause your mind to wander or lose focus. Pay attention to what you think. If you will use Philippians 4:8 as a guide, you will find yourself thinking thoughts that will build you up and not tear you down. As you begin that process of building a positive stronghold, the negative one will crumble and you will eventually find your mind—and your mouth—completely transformed in uplifting, life-giving ways.

CHAPTER 19

Give a Good Report

During Old Testament times, God's people, Israel, were aware of the Promised Land He said He would give them. They may not have been aware of the difficulties involved in getting there. In fact, at times, their own attitudes, words, and actions made their journey much harder and longer than it had to be. When they finally got close, their leader, Moses, sent twelve spies into the land to find out what would be involved in possessing this promised place. Numbers 13:32 tells us what ten of the spies concluded: "So they brought the Israelites an evil report of the land which they had scouted out, saying, The land through which we went to spy it out is a land that devours its inhabitants. And all the people that we saw in it are men of great stature."

That was *not* a good report! It was so discouraging and frightening to the people of Israel that they began to weep and grumble. They even talked about choosing a new leader and going back to slavery in Egypt (Numbers

14:1–4). Think about it: One negative report influenced an entire nation in such a bad way that they wanted to totally give up on God's promise. They wanted to return to back-breaking labor and harsh submission to the Egyptians— just because of what a small group of people had said!

But Moses had sent twelve spies into the land, and two of them, Joshua and Caleb, gave an entirely different report from the one the ten had given. They said, "The land through which we passed as scouts is an exceedingly good land. If the Lord delights in us, then He will bring us into this land and give it to us, a land flowing with milk and honey" (Numbers 14:7–8).

What a difference! The ten spies gave a totally depressing report, while Joshua and Caleb spoke extremely positively, with faith and courage, about the very same place the ten spies thought was so bad. This emphasizes the point that many situations in life have both positive and negative aspects and that the way we view things determines whether those situations will intimidate and defeat us or whether we will conquer them with God's help.

The ten spies spoke negatively about the Promised Land because they viewed it negatively. They chose not to see the positive aspects of it or the possibilities in it.

I'm sure the Promised Land was like anything else people encounter; it had its pluses and its minuses. I doubt every single thing about it was perfect, because nothing on earth is perfect. No matter how we wish we could deal with perfect people, work at perfect jobs, live in perfect neighborhoods, attend perfect churches, or manage our time or money perfectly, the fact is that nothing is without its flaws or challenges. Every person we encounter and every circumstance is a mixed bag of things we like and things we do not like. God does not want us to focus on the bad; He wants us to magnify the good.

As I mentioned earlier, when I write about focusing on the positive, I am not talking about closing our eyes to the legitimately bad things in life and never acknowledging or dealing with them. My point is that we can live in reality and see things as they are and choose to view them with an optimistic perspective, think positive thoughts about them, and give good reports concerning them.

The truth is, no matter how bad a situation may be, speaking negatively about it will not change it. When we speak badly about it to ourselves, we only push ourselves further into negativity. When we complain to others or use our prayer times to moan and groan to God, we make things worse.

The only way to make a situation better is to go to God honestly and ask Him to intervene. We do not have to deny what may be wrong, but we do need to demonstrate our willingness to see the good in it and confess our trust in God to change it as He sees fit. We could say something like this: "God, I'm hurting right now because of my circumstances, but I know You have a great plan for my life and I know You are moving me toward it. I believe You can use this situation for my good, and I trust You to turn it around and make it a blessing in my life."

I certainly don't think we should never mention the problems or struggles we face. Sometimes, simply letting a mature friend or a counselor know what we are going through can be very helpful. In addition, if we know someone who has the power to change our situation, we might speak with that person about it. But simply talking about our troubles for no reason other than to just talk will not solve anything. If we are going to talk about our problems, we should do so with the goal of making the situation better, not worse.

Go back to the story of the ten negative Hebrew spies who scouted out the Promised Land; nothing they said to Moses was positive. They acknowledged the milk and honey, as did Joshua and Caleb, but then their report quickly turned negative:

> *They told Moses, We came to the land to which you sent us; surely it flows with milk and honey. This is its fruit. But the people who dwell there are strong, and the cities are fortified and very large; moreover, there we saw the sons of Anak [of great stature and courage].*
>
> Numbers 13:27–28

The spies then went on to say that various enemies of the Israelites dwelled in certain parts of the Promised

Land. The people began to grumble and complain about this, but Caleb spoke up and calmed them down. Then, without denying the presence of their enemies, he said, "Let us go up at once and possess it; we are well able to conquer it" (Numbers 13:30).

The ten spies spoke doubt and fear, while Caleb, speaking for himself and Joshua, spoke faith, courage, and victory. As a result, Joshua and Caleb were the only two of the twelve spies allowed to enter the Promised Land. The other spies died in the wilderness along with the Israelites who chose to believe the negative report.

In Matthew 12:36, Jesus says, "But I tell you, on the day of judgment men will have to give account for every idle (inoperative, nonworking) word they speak." If certain things we say can be "nonworking," then other things can be "working." In other words, what we say with our mouths makes a difference. Our words either work for us or against us.

We need to keep in mind the power or working ability of our words every time we open our mouths to speak. The ten Hebrew spies failed to do this, and they missed out on God's promise.

No matter what you face, always believe God's promises. Even if you have to overcome some difficulties in order to see those promises come to pass, speak positively about them. Put the words of your mouth to work in your life through speaking hope, faith, courage, and breakthrough.

PART 5

YOUR WORDS CAN DETERMINE YOUR FUTURE

CHAPTER 20

Believe and Speak

God has a great plan for your life. He says in Jeremiah 29:11, "For I know the thoughts and plans that I have for you, says the Lord, thoughts and plans for welfare and peace and not for evil, to give you hope in your final outcome."

This good plan is already established in the spiritual realm, but the enemy works hard to interrupt and destroy it. Unfortunately, he has had a high rate of success in many people's lives. Jesus has come to destroy the works of the enemy (1 John 3:8) and make a way for God's good plans to manifest in our lives.

We will not see positive results in our daily lives if we consistently speak negative things. When we speak something, we are actually calling it forth. We are reaching into the spiritual realm and drawing things out according to our words. Every time we open our mouths, we can choose to reach into the enemy's camp—the realm of curses—and draw out negative things, or we can reach into God's territory—the realm of blessings—and draw out positive things. The choice is ours.

A person may believe for many things and yet see very little manifestation of them. One major reason for this may be that they do not understand the powerful connection between believing and speaking. The best way to demonstrate our belief in what God says and what God has planned for us is to talk about it. Normally, the more strongly we believe in something, the more likely we are to talk about it. So, it stands to reason that if we say we believe in God and yet we never talk about Him that our believing may not be very strong. Or, if we say we believe God will meet our need and yet we continually talk about how worried we are about our troubles, then we probably have weak believing at best.

When God created the world, He gave us a great example of believing then speaking what He believed into existence. God believed there could be light and He said, "Let there be light" (Genesis 1:3). While the Bible does not give us direct insight into God's thought processes in creation, we know what He was thinking because we see what He created. Throughout the first chapter of Genesis, we read that everything God made came into existence when He spoke (Genesis 1:3, 6, 7, 9, 11, 14, 15, 20, 24, 26). From the very beginning of Scripture, this principle of speaking and manifestation is established.

Hebrews 11:3 reminds us of this, saying, "By faith we understand that the worlds were framed *by the word of*

God…" (NKJV, emphasis mine). Several chapters before this, in Hebrews 1:3, we read that everything God created in the beginning is now being upheld "by the word of His power" (NKJV).

Clearly, God operates according to the principle of believing and speaking, and He understands the power of words. As mere human beings, we may not achieve this perfectly, as God does, but the Bible does say we are created in His image and it tells us to imitate Him and aim to be like Him (see Genesis 1:26–27; Ephesians 5:1), so we should do our best to follow His example of believing and speaking things into existence.

If we are going to do what God does, we need to understand how He operates. Romans 4:17 says God "gives life to the dead and speaks of the nonexistent things that [He has foretold and promised] as if they [already] existed."

God's Word is His promise to us, and we should talk about the things He has promised us as though they already exist. When we choose to believe and speak God's Word and live in agreement with Him, we experience God's power and joy in our lives.

There is a great deal of hopelessness in the world today, but with God there is always hope. Our hope is in Him and in His promises, so it stands to reason that the more we talk of His promises, the more hopeful we will be. Psalm 71:5 says, "For You are my hope; O Lord God, You are my trust from my youth and the source of my confidence."

Let's imagine that some individuals have lost their jobs

and they are in great need financially. What will be the most helpful to them? Would it be better to be fearful, worried, and anxious, verbalizing all of their concerns, or would it be better to recall and confess the many promises in God's Word that He will meet our needs? These people don't have to deny that they have a need, but they also have the privilege as God's children to verbalize their trust in Him and His Word. The psalmist David was very honest about his feelings, and yet he always turned to God's Word for strength and comfort: "This is my comfort and consolation in my affliction: that Your word has revived me and given me life" (Psalm 119:50).

If we choose to fill our conversation with God's promises, it will revive, strengthen, and encourage us, but if we only speak of our troubles and fears, it will weaken and discourage us.

In our times of darkness we, too, can say, "Let there be light. Let all the goodness of God come into my life and overtake the darkness."

Let us remember that what is in our hearts will ultimately come out of our mouths (Matthew 12:34). We believe and then we speak. Let your mind be renewed with God's Word and then speak in agreement with and get excited about the wonderful things you will experience because of God's great grace.

CHAPTER 21

Prophesy Your Future

I believe God is looking for people in whom to plant His "dream seeds" for the future. But in order to carry out God's dreams for our lives and for the lives of others, we must be willing to "conceive" a dream. We must see with our spiritual eyes what God wants to do in our natural lives. This means we must be willing to mentally agree with God, to believe what He tells us, just as Abraham believed the seemingly impossible promise that he and his elderly wife would have a biological son (see Genesis 15:1–6).

Believing is the first important step to conceiving and fulfilling a dream, and then what we believe in our hearts will come out of our mouths.

Many of us do not use our mouths for the purposes for which God gave them to us. As I have said before, there is great power and authority in words. The kind of power that gets released in our lives depends on the kind of words we speak. We can curse our future by speaking evil of it, or we can bless it by speaking well of it.

So let me ask you: How do you talk about your future? If you are not satisfied with your life and you want to see it change, you will have to begin speaking a better future for yourself and your loved ones according to God's Word.

A basic principle of God's method of operation is this: First He declares things; then He does them. In the following passage, we see that God wanted Israel to know that He was going to do great works in their lives, so He announced these things ahead of time. In Isaiah 48:3, 5–7, God says:

> *I have declared from the beginning the former things [which happened in times past to Israel]; they went forth from My mouth and I made them known; then suddenly I did them, and they came to pass [says the Lord] . . .*
>
> *Therefore I have declared things to come to you from of old; before they came to pass I announced them to you, so that you could not say, My idol has done them, and my graven image and my molten image have commanded them. You have heard [these things foretold], now you see this fulfillment. And will you not bear witness to it? I show you specified new things from this time forth, even hidden things [kept in reserve] which you have not known. They are created now [called into being by the prophetic word], and not long ago; and before today you have never heard of them, lest you should say, Behold, I knew them!*

God is saying that the things He desired to do were called into being by the prophetic word. In other words, prophecies bring forth realities. This explains why God sent the prophets. They came speaking God-inspired, God-instructed words on the earth that brought forth God's will from the spiritual realm into the natural realm. Jesus did not come to earth until first the prophets had spoken about Him for hundreds of years.

Because God operates through spiritual laws that He has set in place, we cannot ignore them. And because we are created in God's image, we can follow His example and do what He does. So, this is what you and I are to do: Speak forth and declare the Word of the Lord *before* it comes to pass. We, too, can prophesy things to come, good things in the days ahead.

"But I'm no prophet," you might say.

You don't have to function in the office of a prophet in order to prophesy. When the Spirit of God lives in you, you can prophesy, or speak forth, God's Word over your life at any time.

Be encouraged that you *can* change things in your life by cooperating with God. Without God, you cannot change anything, but in agreement with Him, all things are possible (see Matthew 19:26; Mark 9:23). I have experienced this personally and have seen it happen more times than I can count in other people's lives, so I know that you can begin to change things if you will take the Word of God and start speaking it over your life.

By now, you are aware of the danger of speaking negatively, but God does not want you to stop with simply knowing that. He wants you to go beyond that and begin to prophesy (speak forth) what you desire to see happen in your life that God has promised you in His Word.

Please understand: When I encourage you to prophesy your future, I am not talking about telling others what you believe you are going to do or have. There may be a time for that, but not at this stage. I am talking about prophesying to yourself first: while driving to work, cleaning house, or doing other things as part of your daily routine. Begin to talk to yourself about the promises of God you are expecting to manifest in your life, and keep it between you and God until He leads you to share it with someone else.

Let God's promises incubate in your spirit and eventually you will give birth to the dreams He has placed in your heart. I believed for many years that someday I would teach God's Word around the world, and today that is a reality. In the beginning, however, I saw no visible sign of my dream coming to pass. Other than God, I was the only one who believed it. I prayed about it; I prepared to teach by studying God's Word diligently; I thought about doing it; and I spoke of it aloud when I was alone with God. Along the way, small things happened that encouraged me to keep believing, and then eventually I was living my dream.

What is incubating inside of you? What do you think

about most of the time? What do you talk about most of the time? Believe that God can and will do great things through you and with you. Dream big because we serve a big God!

I know a mom with a little boy who doesn't have much interest in talking. If he wants something, he often cries, or grunts, or points at what he wants, but his mom won't give it to him until he uses his words. She frequently tells him, "Use your words." Perhaps that is what God is saying to us. God has given us His Word; now it is time for us to use our words and watch the results!

———

CHAPTER 22

Use Your Words to Cooperate with God's Plan

The Lord wants you to see that He knows from the beginning how things will turn out in the end. Take a look at what He says about this in Isaiah 46:9–10:

> *I am God, and there is no one else; I am God, and there is none like Me, declaring the end and the result from the beginning, and from ancient times the things that are not yet done, saying, My counsel shall stand, and I will do all My pleasure and purpose.*

The Lord is the Alpha and the Omega, the Beginning and the End (see Revelation 1:8). He is also everything in between. He knows before trouble ever shows up that we can be victorious if we fight the battle His way. His way is not a negative way.

Romans 8:37 says that we are "more than conquerors." I believe that means we can know before the battle ever begins that we will win. In other words, we can see the end from the beginning. We have read God's promises and we believe them!

Prophesying our future is literally declaring in the beginning what will happen in the end. This includes declaring with our words our dreams and visions for the future about every aspect of our lives. There are blessings we desire in many realms—personal, spiritual, relational, financial—for our families, our careers, our health, and in many other areas.

There were times in my life when I desired things that would have fallen under the category of "blessings." But because I did not understand the power of my words, I made comments such as, "I will probably never have this," or "Because of my past, I don't think I can ever experience that." I talked about my future based on what my experience had been in the past, and therefore I cursed my future with my own words. I was agreeing with the devil instead of with God, Who always gives us hope for our future (Jeremiah 29:11).

I needed to learn to call things that were not as though they were (Romans 4:17). I had to learn to call forth from the spiritual realm what I desired and believed could and would happen, even though in the present it was not a reality yet.

I also had to learn to cooperate with God's good plan for my life, but I could not do that because I was deceived. I believed the enemy's lies instead of God's truth. Satan is called the deceiver because, as Jesus said in John 8:44, he is a liar and the father of all that is false. He works to cause trouble for us and then uses it to make us think in ways that lead us to prophesy that same kind of past trouble into our future. He is a master at making us believe things will never change, but God is always ready to lead us into different, wonderful experiences and accomplishments, and He is a master at making all things new (2 Corinthians 5:17).

Isaiah 65:16–17 gives us great insight into the power of our words:

> *So that he who blesses himself in the earth shall bless himself in the God of truth; and he who swears in the earth shall swear by the God of truth; because the former troubles are forgotten, and because they are hidden from My eyes. For behold, I create new heavens and a new earth; and the former shall not be remembered or come to mind.* (NKJV)

In the above passage, God Himself sets forth a twofold principle we can apply to every area of life where we need a breakthrough. First, we see that no one's words have as much authority in our lives as our own words. Second, we see that our future cannot be blessed until we let go of the past. God makes the same point in Isaiah 43:18–19:

> *Do not [earnestly] remember the former things; neither consider the things of old. Behold, I am doing a new*

thing! Now it springs forth; do you not perceive and know it and will you not give heed to it? I will even make a way in the wilderness and rivers in the desert.

These two passages from Isaiah indicate that you and I can cooperate with God's plan, meaning that we have the ability to work with it. Note that Isaiah 43:19 asks: "Will you not give heed to it?" In other words, we have a choice. We can decide whether to embrace new things in the future or not.

We can release God's plan for our lives by no longer thinking about the past but believing that God has a good plan for our future.

I believe that if we stop mentally living in the past, we can begin to think in agreement with God about our future. Once our thoughts align with God's thoughts, we can bring our words into agreement with His words.

If you are like many people, you are ready and waiting for some new things to happen in your life. God says in Isaiah 42:9: "Behold, the former things have come to pass, and new things I now declare; before they spring forth I tell you of them."

If you are tired of the old things in your life, then stop speaking the old things. If you want some new things, then start speaking new things. Find out what His will is for your life by studying His Word and begin to declare it out of your mouth. Don't let the enemy, or your own carnal thoughts and emotions, guide your life anymore or keep you bound to the past. Start speaking the new things God has for you. Instead of saying, "Nothing will ever change," say, "Good changes are taking place in my life and circumstances every day." Find out what God's Word promises you and begin to declare the end from the beginning as you use your words to agree and cooperate with God's plan for your future.

———

CHAPTER 23

See It, Say It

In order to prophesy our future, we must know what God has said and is saying to us, and we must believe it, even if we do not see it happening right away. If anyone in the Bible can be given credit for believing God without seeing any manifestation of God's Word, it is Abraham (once called Abram). Let me remind you of his story, using Genesis 15:1–6:

> *After these things, the word of the Lord came to Abram in a vision, saying, Fear not, Abram, I am your Shield, your abundant compensation, and your reward shall be exceedingly great. And Abram said, Lord God, what can You give me, since I am going on [from this world] childless and he who shall be the owner and heir of my house is this [steward] Eliezer of Damascus? And Abram continued, Look, You have given me no child; and [a servant] born in my house is my heir. And behold, the word of the Lord came to him, saying,*

*This man shall not be your heir, but he who shall come
from your own body shall be your heir. And He brought
him outside [his tent into the starlight] and said, Look
now toward the heavens and count the stars—if you
are able to number them. Then He said to him, So shall
your descendants be. And he [Abram] believed in (trusted
in, relied on, remained steadfast to) the Lord, and
He counted it to him as righteousness (right standing
with God).*

Abraham is often referred to as the "father of faith," and
this is because he never doubted or wavered in his belief
that a seemingly impossible promise from God would
come to pass. In his early years, Abraham was known as
Abram, and his wife, Sarah, was known as Sarai. They
were childless, and definitely beyond childbearing years.
But they received a promise from God that He would give
them a child of their own, a child from their own bodies.
That would take a miracle!

God said to them in Genesis 17:5, 15–16:

*Nor shall your name any longer be Abram [high,
exalted father]; but your name shall be Abraham
[father of a multitude], for I have made you the father
of many nations…And God said to Abraham, As for
Sarai your wife, you shall not call her name Sarai; but
Sarah [Princess] her name shall be. And I will bless her
and give you a son also by her. Yes, I will bless her, and*

*she shall be a mother of nations; kings of peoples shall
come from her.*

Perhaps God changed their names because Abram and
Sarai needed new names before that miracle could occur.
Their new names had special meanings. Each time their
names were called, their future was being prophesied:
Abraham would be the father of a multitude, and his prin-
cess, Sarah, would be the mother of nations and kings.

I doubt that childless Sarai had an image of herself
as a princess. In her day, barren women were not highly
regarded and she was no doubt aware of the stigma she
carried. She needed to see herself differently, and receiving
a new name was an important part of that new self-image.

Once the right things were being declared over Abram
and Sarai through the changing of their names, their
promised future began to unfold. With those new names,
words were being spoken into the atmosphere and were
reaching into the spiritual realm, where Abraham and
Sarah's miracle existed. Every time those words were
said, they began to call forth and draw out the miracle
God had promised. At that point, the words on earth were
coming into agreement with God's Word, as He spoke it
in Genesis 15.

The key to the fulfillment of God's promise to Abraham was that Abraham *believed* what God told him. Even
the apostle Paul, who lived much later than Abraham,
wrote about Abraham's great faith in Romans 4:18–21:

[For Abraham, human reason for] hope being gone, hoped in faith that he should become the father of many nations, as he had been promised, So [numberless] shall your descendants be. He did not weaken in faith when he considered the [utter] impotence of his own body, which was as good as dead because he was about a hundred years old, or [when he considered] the barrenness of Sarah's [deadened] womb. No unbelief or distrust made him waver (doubtingly question) concerning the promise of God, but he grew strong and was empowered by faith as he gave praise and glory to God fully satisfied and assured that God was able and mighty to keep His word and to do what He had promised.

Like Abraham, we will not receive a miracle unless we believe that God can do the impossible and that He will do it for us.

In Abraham's case, the promised miracle did not occur immediately. Many years passed between the time God told him he would be the father of many nations and the birth of his son Isaac.

Not only did Abraham and Sarah believe God, but the words of their mouths also helped release their faith. The Amplified Bible's rendering of Romans 4:17 says we serve a God Who "speaks of the nonexistent things that [He has foretold and promised] as if they [already] existed." Based on Romans 4:18–21, I believe this is what Abraham did.

Prophesying our future by speaking in agreement with

God's Word, whether it is His written Word or a specific word He has given us by His Spirit, helps keep our faith strong until we see God's promise come to pass.

Let your mouth be filled with faith, not doubt and unbelief. Be positive at all times. You can be positive even when your circumstances are rather negative. Don't deny the reality of a problem, but deny it the right to control your mood and attitude. Jesus said that in the world we would have tribulation, but He instructs us to *"cheer up"* because He has overcome the world (John 16:33). Put a smile on your face, fill your mind with good things, and speak words that agree with God!

In this book, I have tried to emphasize how much blessing—and how much damage—we can do with the words of our mouths. I have also tried to explain how the process of spiritual growth and preparation for God to use us involves learning to change the way we speak.

I hope you will remember all the key principles and truths in this book, but if you only remember one, make it this: *Words are containers for power.* That is why the Bible includes so many passages on the proper and improper use of our mouths.

To illustrate many of the Scripture verses and passages related to the mouth, I have shared several personal experiences highlighting the lessons I have learned in my own life and ministry. I have also tried to help you know how to apply these truths from God's Word to your own everyday life.

At the end of this book, in the appendices, I have included three different types of confessions so you can easily reference them and get into the habit of speaking God's Word often. The first appendix covers general faith-building confessions from the Bible. The second provides you with Scriptures on the power of your words, and the third gives you a list of reminders of how powerful God's Word is. I have used many of these confessions for years to apply God's Word to many situations all of us face in our Christian walk.

My sincere prayer is that these will help you in your effort to gain control over your words, and thus change your circumstances and your life—for your own sake and for the sake of the people with whom you come in contact.

Let me encourage you in the same way 2 Timothy 2:16 urges all of us: "But avoid all empty (vain, useless, idle) talk, for it will lead people into more and more ungodliness." Instead, learn to speak as God speaks. It is the Word of God, spoken in truth and with love from your lips, that will return to Him after accomplishing His will and purpose (see Isaiah 55:11).

But in order to speak that Word in truth and love, your heart must be right before the Lord, because it is out of the abundance of the heart that the mouth speaks—for good or evil (Matthew 12:34–35).

We are bound by our words; we are also judged by them (Matthew 12:37). That is why placing a guard upon your lips (Psalm 141:3) is so important—so that what comes forth from them is not only truthful, but also kind, positive, and in line with the will of God.

Any of us can change our actions and behaviors, but to do so we must first change our thoughts and words.

And the only way we can do that is with the help of God's Spirit, Who lives within us.

If you want your life to be totally different, let me encourage you to submit yourself to God and humbly ask Him to transform you into the nature and image of His Son Jesus Christ.

He is doing that for me, and He will do it for you, too. God wants your words to reflect His Word and His heart. As that happens more and more, you will see His power increase in your life.

God bless you.

Confessions from the Word of God

When we confess the Word of God, we help establish its truths in our hearts. The list below includes some of the confessions I spoke for six months, twice a day, when I was first learning to confess the Word. By that time, I had spoken them so often that they had become part of me. To this day, many years later, I still hear many of these same words come out of my mouth when I am praying. In addition to that, I can look at my list of confessions now and am absolutely amazed when I think about how impossible some of those things seemed when I first began to speak them and how many of them have now come to pass. I believe the same thing will happen in your life as you believe and confess God's Word.

I am a new creation in Christ:

Therefore, if anyone is in Christ, he is a new creation; old things have passed away; behold, all things have become new.

2 Corinthians 5:17, NKJV

I am dead to sin, but alive to righteousness in Christ Jesus:

Reckon yourselves to be dead indeed to sin, but alive to God in Christ Jesus our Lord.

Romans 6:11, NKJV

Who Himself bore our sins in His own body on the tree, that we, having died to sins, might live for righteousness.

1 Peter 2:24, NKJV

I know the truth and the truth sets me free:

And you shall know the truth, and the truth shall make you free.

John 8:32, NKJV

Therefore if the Son makes you free, you shall be free indeed.

John 8:36, NKJV

**The love of God has been shed abroad
in my heart:**

> *The love of God is shed abroad in our hearts by the
> Holy Ghost which is given unto us.*
>
> Romans 5:5, KJV

**I do all my work excellently and with
great prudence:**

> *Whatever your hand finds to do, do it with your might.*
>
> Ecclesiastes 9:10, NKJV

> *Do you see a man who excels in his work? He will stand
> before kings; he will not stand before unknown men.*
>
> Proverbs 22:29, NKJV

I use my time wisely:

> *See then that you walk circumspectly, not as fools
> but as wise, redeeming the time, because the days are
> evil.*
>
> Ephesians 5:15–16, NKJV

**I cast all my care upon the Lord,
for He cares for me:**

> *Casting all your care upon Him, for He cares for you.*
>
> 1 Peter 5:7, NKJV

**I do not have a spirit of fear, but of power
and of love and of a sound mind:**

> *For God has not given us a spirit of fear, but of power
> and of love and of a sound mind.*
>
> 2 Timothy 1:7, NKJV

I do not feel guilty or condemned:

> *There is therefore now no condemnation to those who
> are in Christ Jesus, who do not walk according to the
> flesh, but according to the Spirit.*
>
> Romans 8:1, NKJV

**I take every thought captive unto the
obedience of Jesus Christ:**

> *Casting down imaginations, and every high thing that
> exalteth itself against the knowledge of God, and bringing
> into captivity every thought to the obedience of Christ.*
>
> 2 Corinthians 10:5, KJV

**I don't give the enemy a foothold in my life.
I resist the devil and he has to flee from me:**

> *Leave no [such] room or foothold for the devil [give
> no opportunity to him].*
>
> Ephesians 4:27, AMP

> *So be subject to God. Resist the devil [stand firm
> against him], and he will flee from you.*
>
> James 4:7, AMP

No weapon that is formed against me shall prosper,
but every tongue that rises against me in judgment,
I shall show to be in the wrong:

> *But no weapon that is formed against you shall pros-*
> *per, and every tongue that shall rise against you in*
> *judgment you shall show to be in the wrong.*
>
> Isaiah 54:17, AMP

I do not think of myself more highly than
I ought to in the flesh:

> *For I say, through the grace given to me, to everyone*
> *who is among you, not to think of himself more highly*
> *than he ought to think, but to think soberly, as God has*
> *dealt to each one a measure of faith.*
>
> Romans 12:3, NKJV

I am quick to hear, slow to speak,
and slow to anger:

> *Let every man be swift to hear, slow to speak, slow to*
> *wrath.*
>
> James 1:19, NKJV

I have purposed that my mouth shall not transgress.
I will speak forth the righteousness and
praise of God all the day long:

> *I have purposed that my mouth shall not transgress.*
>
> Psalm 17:3, NKJV

And my tongue shall speak of Your righteousness and of Your praise all the day long.

Psalm 35:28, NKJV

The law of kindness is in my tongue. Gentleness is in my touch. Mercy and compassion are in my hearing:

On her tongue is the law of kindness.

Proverbs 31:26, NKJV

We were gentle among you, just as a nursing mother cherishes her own children.

1 Thessalonians 2:7, NKJV

Show mercy and compassion everyone to his brother.

Zechariah 7:9, NKJV

I am a positive encourager. I edify people and build them up. I do not tear them down or destroy them:

Let each one of us make it a practice to please (make happy) his neighbor for his good and for his true welfare, to edify him [to strengthen him and build him up spiritually].

Romans 15:2, AMP

I cry to God Most High Who performs
on my behalf and rewards me:

> I will cry to God Most High, Who performs on my
> behalf and rewards me [Who brings to pass His pur-
> poses for me and surely completes them].

Psalm 57:2, AMP

I am a giver. It is more blessed to give than to
receive. I love to give! I have plenty of
money to give away all the time:

> Remember the words of the Lord Jesus, that He said, "It
> is more blessed to give than to receive."

Acts 20:35, NKJV

> So let each one give as he purposes in his heart, not
> grudgingly or of necessity; for God loves a cheerful
> giver. And God is able to make all grace abound toward
> you, that you, always having all sufficiency in all
> things, may have an abundance for every good work.

2 Corinthians 9:7–8, NKJV

All the members of my household are blessed. We are
blessed when we come in and when we go out:

> Blessed shall be the fruit of your body … blessed shall
> you be when you come in, and blessed shall you be
> when you go out.

Deuteronomy 28:4, 6, NKJV

Scriptures to Remind You of the Power of Your Words

Anytime you need to be reminded of how powerful your words are, read, study, and meditate on these Scriptures.

> *Let the words of my mouth and the meditation of my heart be acceptable in Your sight. O Lord, my [firm, impenetrable] Rock and my Redeemer.*
>
> Psalm 19:14

> *Keep your tongue from evil and your lips from speaking deceit.*
>
> Psalm 34:13

> *The mouth of the [uncompromisingly] righteous man is a well of life, but the mouth of the wicked conceals violence.*
>
> Proverbs 10:11

He who guards his mouth keeps his life, but he who opens wide his lips comes to ruin.

Proverbs 13:3

A soft answer turns away wrath, but grievous words stir up anger.

Proverbs 15:1

A gentle tongue [with its healing power] is a tree of life, but willful contrariness in it breaks down the spirit.

Proverbs 15:4

A man has joy in making an apt answer, and a word spoken at the right moment—how good it is!

Proverbs 15:23

The mind of the wise instructs his mouth, and adds learning and persuasiveness to his lips.

Proverbs 16:23

Pleasant words are as a honeycomb, sweet to the mind and healing to the body.

Proverbs 16:24

Death and life are in the power of the tongue, and they who indulge in it shall eat the fruit of it [for death or life].

Proverbs 18:21

A word fitly spoken and in due season is like apples of gold in settings of silver.

Proverbs 25:11

[The Servant of God says] the Lord God has given Me the tongue of a disciple and of one who is taught, that I should know how to speak a word in season to him who is weary. He wakens Me morning by morning. He wakens My ear to hear as a disciple [as one who is taught].

Isaiah 50:4

Out of the fullness (the overflow, the superabundance) of the heart the mouth speaks. The good man from his inner good treasure flings forth good things, and the evil man out of his inner evil storehouse flings forth evil things. But I tell you, on the day of judgment men will have to give account for every idle (inoperative, nonworking) word they speak. For by your words you will be justified and acquitted, and by your words you will be condemned and sentenced.

Matthew 12:34–37

Let no foul or polluting language, nor evil word nor unwholesome or worthless talk [ever] come out of your mouth, but only such speech as is good and beneficial to the spiritual progress of others, as is fitting to the need and the occasion, that it may be a blessing and give grace (God's favor) to those who hear it.

Ephesians 4:29

Let your speech at all times be gracious (pleasant and winsome), seasoned [as it were] with salt, [so that you may never be at a loss] to know how you ought to answer anyone [who puts a question to you].

Colossians 4:6

For our [preaching of the] glad tidings (the Gospel) came to you not only in word, but also in [its own inherent] power and in the Holy Spirit and with great conviction and absolute certainty [on our part].

1 Thessalonians 1:5

For let him who wants to enjoy life and see good days [good—whether apparent or not] keep his tongue free from evil and his lips from guile (treachery, deceit).

1 Peter 3:10

Scriptures on the Power of Confessing God's Word

This Book of the Law shall not depart out of your mouth, but you shall meditate on it day and night, that you may observe and do according to all that is written in it. For then you shall make your way prosperous, and then you shall deal wisely and have good success.

Joshua 1:8

Your word is a lamp to my feet and a light to my path.

Psalm 119:105

So shall My Word be that goes forth out of My mouth: it shall not return to Me void [without producing any effect, useless], but it shall accomplish that which I please and purpose, and it shall prosper in the thing for which I sent it.

Isaiah 55:11

So [it shall be] that he who invokes a blessing on him-self in the land shall do so by saying, May the God of truth and fidelity [the Amen] bless me; and he who takes an oath in the land shall swear by the God of truth and faithfulness to His promises [the Amen], because the former troubles are forgotten and because they are hidden from My eyes.

Isaiah 65:16

Then the Lord said to me, You have seen well, for I am alert and active, watching over My word to perform it.

Jeremiah 1:12

Truly I tell you, whoever says to this mountain, Be lifted up and thrown into the sea! and does not doubt at all in his heart but believes that what he says will take place, it will be done for him.

Mark 11:23

The Word (God's message in Christ) is near you, on your lips and in your heart; that is, the Word (the message, the basis and object) of faith which we preach, because if you acknowledge and confess with your lips that Jesus is Lord and in your heart believe (adhere to, trust in, and rely on the truth) that God raised Him from the dead, you will be saved.

Romans 10:8–9

*For the Word that God speaks is alive and full of power
[making it active, operative, energizing, and effective];
it is sharper than any two-edged sword, penetrating
to the dividing line of the breath of life (soul) and [the
immortal] spirit, and of joints and marrow [of the
deepest parts of our nature], exposing and sifting and
analyzing and judging the very thoughts and purposes
of the heart.*

Hebrews 4:12

*Inasmuch then as we have a great High Priest Who has
[already] ascended and passed through the heavens,
Jesus the Son of God, let us hold fast our confession [of
faith in Him].*

Hebrews 4:14

*So let us seize and hold fast and retain without waver-
ing the hope we cherish and confess and our acknowl-
edgement of it, for He Who promised is reliable (sure)
and faithful to His word.*

Hebrews 10:23

JOYCE MEYER is one of the world's leading practical Bible teachers. Her daily broadcast, *Enjoying Everyday Life*, airs on hundreds of television networks and radio stations worldwide.

Joyce has written more than one hundred inspirational books. Her bestsellers include *Power Thoughts*; *The Confident Woman*; *Look Great, Feel Great*; *Starting Your Day Right*; *Ending Your Day Right*; *Approval Addiction*; *How to Hear from God*; *Beauty for Ashes*; and *Battlefield of the Mind*.

Joyce travels extensively, holding conferences throughout the year and speaking to thousands around the world.

Joyce Meyer Ministries
P.O. Box 655
Fenton, MO 63026
USA
(636) 349-0303

Joyce Meyer Ministries—Canada
P.O. Box 7700
Vancouver, BC V6B 4E2
Canada
(800) 868-1002

Joyce Meyer Ministries—Australia
Locked Bag 77
Mansfield Delivery Centre
Queensland 4122
Australia
(07) 3349 1200

Joyce Meyer Ministries—England
P.O. Box 1549
Windsor SL4 1GT
United Kingdom
01753 831102

Joyce Meyer Ministries—South Africa
P.O. Box 5
Cape Town 8000
South Africa
(27) 21-701-1056

OTHER BOOKS BY JOYCE MEYER